D0879658

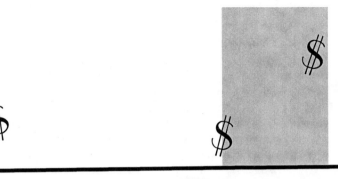

How To Make Big
Money Mowing Small Lawns

For Teens, Retirees, and
Anyone in Between

"The Classic Book"
To start and operate a lawn mowing business

ROBERT A. WELCOME

authorHOUSE®

AuthorHouse™
1663 Liberty Drive, Suite 200
Bloomington, IN 47403
www.authorhouse.com
Phone: 1-800-839-8640

Fourth Edition
First printing, September 1984
Second printing, April 1997
Third printing, May 2005
Fourth printing, January 2008
First published by AuthorHouse   5/21/2008

ISBN: 978-1-4343-7226-0 (e)
ISBN: 978-1-4343-7033-4 (sc)

Library of Congress Catalog Card Number: 84-90998

Printed in the United States of America
Bloomington, Indiana

This book is printed on acid-free paper.

Most of the changes in this fourth edition are associated with costs and prices that have increased since the third edition. These changes, to a great extent, are related to the estimation of prices for mowing jobs. Many of the changes were made, however, without losing the original baseline data.

Reviews

Unexpected offerings from grass roots ...journey to the land of publishing gems, ...some wonderful tips.

San Francisco Chronicle

A lawn mower's route to success.

Charlotte Observer

...presents classic summertime employment...as a profitable and challenging junior business.

Boston Globe (Sunday Magazine)

...guides teens to summer profits.

Springfield Republican

[There are] tables to help the reader make profitable estimates and offers ... field-tested advice.

Miami Herald

Lawn mowing tycoon ...illustrated guide explaining how to start and operate a lawn-mowing business.

Boston Globe

ACKNOWLEDGMENTS

This book is the result of a cooperative effort between the author and his son, John.

Thanks to John for having the motivation to work for himself, part-time, during his high school years and for his cooperative effort to keep making changes that would continually improve upon his little business. Many changes were made by experimenting with marketing, advertising, estimating, pricing, scheduling and all phases of the business; this is quite difficult, even for mature adults.

And, thanks to my wife, John's mother, Janice, for her patience and ability to smooth over the delicate phone calls, when John would occasionally be late, or forget to mow a lawn.

Also, much appreciation to Donna Murphy for her typing services and to Georgia Wirth for her help with typesetting and layout work, for the first edition.

ROBERT A. WELCOME

ABOUT THE AUTHOR
AND HIS SON

Author

Author's Son,
John

The author is a graduate of the University of Massachusetts, with a B.S. Degree (cum laude) in Electrical Engineering. He was employed with GE Aerospace Industries, 30 years, where he enjoyed a wide variety of responsibilities. He was a Design Engineer; a Systems Engineer; a Test-Berth Director; a Cost Analyst; and he held several business development and management positions. He also was the GE Rep to the International Society of Parametric Analyst (ISPA), a prestigious, high-level, corporate appointment to do international analyses and reporting work for both the U.S. Government and GE-related enterprises (associated with the Department of Defense). During his last 15-years of employment he worked on advanced plans and programs and authored many documents for GE and the U.S. Government.

In his private life, he and his wife, Janice, raised three children. The children (Michael, John and Angela) were raised with a sense of knowing what it is to be in their own business. Each of them had their own paper routes. They also shared in a night-crawler sales business and in a business of selling U.S. postage stamps in vending machines in 11 local retail stores. This eventually let to his son John, at age 14, wanting to start a lawn-wowing business. After four years of effort to perfect John's business, and to track and record all the data, this book was written.

AUTHOR'S NOTES

Mowing lawns can be considered as a junior business for teenage part-timers. It can also be considered as a part-time business or stepping-stone business for teenagers, middle-agers, or retirees. Or, it can be considered as a full-fledged business for those who do it exclusively for a living.

For John, the teenager who did the mowing work described in this book, mowing lawns was a part-time venture which also turned out to be a stepping-stone business. In addition to running his mowing business, John learned the basics of investing, marketing, advertising, estimating, pricing, and scheduling; the disciplines of commitment and reliability; and, how to establish good public relations, keep records, and pay taxes. And, he learned these essential aspects of business in a simple, uncomplicated way, as described in the book. Furthermore, he was able to use this knowledge, much to his advantage, later in his adult life.

Since the first edition of this book was printed, John has graduated from high school, served four years in the U. S. Air Force, became a Christian minister, and now operates two businesses: he is a Realtor and a general contractor, building and remodeling homes. His business background from mowing lawns helped to provide him with business foresight toward becoming a contractor; and, in this respect, mowing lawns had become a stepping-stone business for him.

Another young man, "Rick" White formerly of Pittsfield, MA, purchased a copy of the book and went into the mowing business when he graduated from high school. About seven years later (in 1992), I saw "Rick" at a local town fair and asked him what he was doing for work. He told me, with enthusiasm, that he was the proud owner of a large mowing business, and that he had several employees working for him. He also said that when he got started, he "followed the book exactly, to every detail." So, for "Rick", mowing lawns became a full-fledged business.

And, as for retirees: "Russ" White of Lenox, MA (not related to "Rick" White), purchased a copy of the book a few years before he retired and started a part-time mowing business, which he had continued and expanded during his retirement. He says that he "enjoys mowing lawns"; it gives him "plenty of good exercise" and "it pays good, too". He also informed me that his book is barely readable because he let many retirees borrow it, and it has become quite frayed. "Now," he says, "I see quite a few of these guys out mowing lawns,"

For "Russ", and other retirees, mowing lawns is principally a part-time business. It helps them to remain physically active, to have a source of income (without tight schedules) that can appreciably supplement their pensions, and it helps to promote a greater sense of independence.

In addition, this book has been used in various Trade Schools. Also, at Purdue University. Purdue used it in their Landscaping course for students who have abundant technical knowledge about all kinds of plants; but, according to Professor Glen Voris, they lack the "know-how" about how to build a business.

The original reason for writing this book was to have it be available mainly to high school and college students, to help them with employment during the summer vacation period. Sales data from the first edition, however, have shown the scope of interest to be much broader than expected. The data (from copies sold throughout the U. S., from the Atlantic to Pacific coasts, and from Florida to as far north as Anchorage, AK) shows the book to be of interest to youths, retirees, and others in between, who intend to go into his/her own business. There is also a very strong interest for parents, grandparents, aunts, uncles, and friends of teenagers and/or young adults to purchase the book as a gift item for birthdays, Christmas, and periods before and during the mowing season.

A broad interest has resulted from the fact that mowing lawns is a simple, straight-forward business, not requiring any high technology skill. And, it stands out as one of the very best low-investment, high-return businesses available. Also, there is personal satisfaction in the work because, upon completion of mowing a lawn, the finished work is immediately noticeable. The pay is quite satisfying as well, which can easily be triple the federal minimum wage rate of pay.

It is of the greatest personal satisfaction to me to know that so many people have found an interest in the book. Therefore, I would like to thank all of you who have purchased a copy. And I hope that you find a good return for your investment.

ROBERT A. WELCOME

FORWARD

Mowing lawns is a highly independent way of life. I have enjoyed earning a comfortable living at it for 22 years.

My business had originally involved doing mowing and rototilling work for the general public. But now I have a select group of customers. They include homeowners with small lawns; small, wealthy, private estates: and some professional business establishments. And my overall work now consists of mowing, fertilizing, planting shrubs and hedges, trimming shrubs and hedges, and rototilling. Most of the work, however, is mowing.

A review of this book has left me with two distinct impressions: One, I wish it had been available to me when I was just getting started. Two, it is a great book for anyone who wants to go into the mowing business. It's a complete guide. Some of the information is of value even to those, like myself, who are well established in the business.

Besides being most informative, the book is written in a style that instills self motivation. There has long been a need for a book like this. It will be a classic for those who want to get started in the mowing business.

PETER COLLINS
GREEN THUMB
Lawn and Garden Service
Lee, MA

CONTENTS

SLOPES OF HOUSE LOTS
REASONS FOR BEING HIRED
TYPES OF WORK
YOUR OWN MOWER
INCOME

STATISTICAL DATA
MOWING TIME
ESTIMATING, STEP ONE
ASKING "THE CUSTOMER" METHOD
EQUIVALENT-SQUARE METHOD
EQUIVALENT-SQUARE, SHORT-CUT METHOD
ACREAGE-MATRIX METHOD
ACREAGE-EQUATION METHOD
ACREAGE MATRIX
ACREAGE - EQUATION FORMULA
BRIEF REVIEW OF STEP ONE
ESTIMATING, STEP TWO
PAYMENTS RECEIVED
HOURLY RATES OF PAY
LOTS LARGER THAN 0.4 ACRES
PRICE ESTIMATING TABLES, GENERAL DESCRIPTION
PRICE ESTIMATING TABLES, DETAILED DESCRIPTION

THE CUSTOMERS
WEATHER EFFECTS
SAMPLE SCHEDULE
MOWINGS PER MONTH:
TIME BETWEEN MOWINGS
SPECIAL NOTATIONS
MODE OF TRANSPORTATION
WORKING INTO A SCHEDULE
BEST TIME TO ADVERTISE
BEST TIME TO BUY A NEW MOWER
KEEPING TRACK OF INCOME
KEEPING TRACK OF EXPENSES
SCHEDULE FORMS

Chapter 1

INTRODUCTION

Mowing lawns is an excellent way to earn money. It's healthy, outside work with plenty of fresh air and good exercise. When done on a part-time basis, there are no tight schedules. Grass can be cut at your own convenience, without interfering with other activities. It's an ideal way to accept responsibility, be appreciated, and get well paid for it.

Cutting grass can be more than just a summertime job. Lawns need to be mowed during the spring, summer, and fall seasons of the year. In northern regions of the United States, an average annual mowing season starts in late April or early May and ends in mid October, nearly a six-month period. As one moves southward from northern regions, the mowing season progressively lengthens. It extends up to approximately a ten-month period in some areas of the Deep South.

So, depending upon where you live in the United States, work is available from six to ten months of the year. There are only a few exceptions. The southern half of Alaska has a short mowing season that varies from three to five months, depending on altitude and location. In Hawaii and at the southern tip of Florida the mowing season is year-round.

GRASS EVERYWHERE

There's an immense amount of grass that needs to be cut. We see lawns at golf courses, cemeteries, schools, parks, and along the sides of roadways. These jobs are for contractors with expensive, fast-cutting mowers. We also see lawns on the properties of homes, apartment houses, professional business buildings, restaurants, and motels. These jobs can be done by anyone using an ordinary rotary lawn mower. They are the easiest jobs to get. They're also highly profitable.

A big part of the mowing market consists of doing lawns for homes. There is an estimated 20,000 square miles of home lawns in the United States; This is enough grass to more than cover the entire area of the states of Delaware, Massachusetts, New Jersey, and Rhode Island. The home lawn market is huge. There's a large demand for mowing services.

America is a nation hungry for all kinds of services. There has been a rapid growth of fast-food restaurants, automotive quick tune-up shops, and speedy exhaust system installation centers. Moreover, we've seen a continual rise in the number of drive-in banks, one-day photo development sheds, and home-cleaning businesses that further contribute to the trend. These types of businesses all appeal to the same drive toward a more service oriented society. People want more leisure time; the movement also includes a great demand for mowing lawns. Projections of market growth for service industries as a whole are expected to increase through the 21st century.

POTENTIAL INCOME

How much money can you make? It will depend on how ambitious you are. If you're ambitious, you can make big money. Prices are charged by the job, not by the hour. However, if figured on an hourly basis, the average pay is far more than the federal minimum wage guideline. It's even reasonable to expect higher hourly earnings than the average working man.

During 1981, when the initial pricing data in this book was being established, the average working man in the United States was earning $7.19 per hour. At this same time the prices for mowing small house lots were yielding an equivalent of about $10 to $12 an hour. Lawn mowing can indeed be highly profitable work. And there's always increased potential for earnings, by expanding and hiring help to work for you at the federal minimum wage.

There are some lawn mowing companies that employ crews of people to tend lawns and have reported incomes of over a million dollars a year. So the sky's the limit. This is a business that can be run either as a one-man operation or as a large enterprise. It can also be done on just a part-time basis. You have the flexibility of operating at any scale desired.

BASIC REQUIREMENTS

Location is not a crucial decision. You can operate directly from your home.

What's more, you won't need a lot of money to get started. The investment in equipment is minimal. Basically, you'll need a lawn mower. And for some jobs, it's not even essential to have your own mower. Sometimes the customer will have one you can use. However, to get the best prices, you should have your own mower. When you are the one providing the mower, you're always able to charge more money for your services. And the customers are willing to pay more.

This is a business that requires only about five percent practical knowledge. The other 95 percent know-how is plain and simple business sense. It's just a matter of understanding the nature of the business, what must be done, and then acting accordingly. Getting started should be fairly easy. Everything you will need to know is covered in the chapters that follow.

You'll find out all the various reasons why different people want to hire you. Knowing these reasons will give you a feeling for what causes the demand for mowing services. This is the easiest way to understand the lawn mowing market. You'll gain rapid insight into the business.

Further revealed are the secrets of how to advertise by using the least expensive and most effective ways to acquire customers. These are simple, tried and proven methods of advertising. They're easily accomplished by anyone, at practically no cost. Therefore, you'll know how to get the jobs. This is one of the keys to success in any service business.

Many examples of lawn mowing jobs are given. Each example contains an interesting collection of statistical data.

The data consists of important information that tells you the size of the house lot, mowing time, price, and the hourly rate of pay. From this data, you'll see how easy it is to operate the business most efficiently. For instance, you'll know which particular sizes of house lots to concentrate on to maximize your income. Certain sizes of properties can be considerably more profitable than others.

To assist you in quoting the right prices, there is information on estimating. Estimating can be done by selecting any one of several different methods of your choice. You'll be shown how to quickly estimate the size of a house lot, the amount of mowing time required, and the most reasonable, profitable prices to charge. Also included is a handy set of price estimating tables.

Once the business starts taking off, it becomes necessary to have a schedule.

Therefore, a system has been developed for doing this with very little effort. The paperwork can be reduced to such a simple procedure that it can be done on a single sheet of paper. All record keeping can be done with ease.

Furthermore, you'll be given the basic rules of safety for using a power mower and also some information on the operation and minor maintenance of a mower. Every business has certain things that one should avoid doing; the mowing business is no different in this respect. So you'll be advised of shortcomings that are associated with such things as mowing large, time-consuming lawns and mowing lawns with steep slopes. You will be prepared to pick and choose the best jobs.

AGE GROUPS

Those who mow lawns include the young, the old, and everyone in between. High school students and college students do it part-time, primarily during the summer recess period. Older people with full-time jobs mow lawns part-time evenings after work and on weekends for additional income.

There are also a few people who, during their early retirement years, do it part-time to supplement their retirement income. And then there are some who mow lawns for full-time employment, either as a one-man operation or as big business with crews of hired help.

Unfortunately, many of those who mow lawns part-time do it under very limited conditions. They do it strictly based on the five percent practical knowledge required to push a mower; it's quite easy to compete with them. They're hardly aware of the other 95 percent business knowledge that would improve their overall efficiency and earnings.

SMALL LAWNS

The book covers all sizes of small house lots up to the point where the lots get to be a little over one-third acre. The cut-off point is at about one-third of an acre for two main reasons: First, it was found that when lot sizes begin to exceed one-third acre, they become much less profitable. Second, the larger lots require making a big investment in expensive equipment to reach the point where they can become profitable.

Therefore, small lawns can be done for a minimum investment and, financially they can offer handsome returns. It was also found that one could break into the small-lawn market without encountering stiff competition from big mowing contractors. The large mowing contractors mainly go after long-term seasonal contracts to mow very large parcels of land.

CENTRAL THEME

The central theme of the book is how, in the simplest way, to get into the lawn-mowing business; how to do it with a minimum investment; and, how to earn the most income per hour of work. The emphasis is placed on a one-man operation working on a part-time basis. This is the best way to get started and know the business. The same fundamentals apply to full-time work, except that there are more customers.

The knowledge that you will acquire from this book is a direct result of three years of primary research. It is purely an outcome of having continually experimented in the open market. All information comes from on-the-job experience.

PERSONAL NOTES

When I was a boy, I mowed lawns. This was during my high school years in the early 1950s. Many years later, after marrying and raising a family, one of my sons, John, at age 14, became interested in mowing lawns. He was eager to provide his own employment opportunity after being upset because no employer was able to give him part-time work -- not until he was of legal age, 16. At first, I thought this would be just a temporary interest of his that would soon fade away. But John persisted, and his level of ambition mounted.

I decided to show concern for his enthusiasm. I gave my approval and encouraged him to get started. It was to be only a small, part-time business, and I was to guide him based on my experience as a boy. After he got a few customers, he wanted more. He also wanted to be paid more money for his work. We didn't know how high a price customers were willing to pay for mowing work; and, therefore, began to experiment with higher prices for each new customer. I was amazed at the money John began to earn. He was making much more money in an hour than many of the local factory workers.

John continually sought my help, and together we gradually improved all aspects of the business. We did so during each mowing season over a three-year period, until everything that had to be done was reasonably

26

well perfected. Every facet of the business was optimized. This was done by always experimenting to find the best methods for marketing, advertising, estimating, pricing, and scheduling -- all phases of the business.

As far as the customers were concerned, John was the only one involved. I remained in the background and provided support for him on general business planning, marketing strategies, scheduling, ideas to be researched, collection of data, and analysis of the data. In a few words, I managed him. But it was John who actually did the work; and, without my physical help, he entirely earned the fruits of his own labor.

Therefore, what has been written in this book can be accomplished by a boy of about age 15 or any older individual. I say 15 because it wasn't until the second mowing season that John began to be most effective at all phases of the business.

Happily, we share our common experience and knowledge with you. We hope that you too can know the sense of independence that comes with self-employment. Mowing lawns is, without question, a genuine opportunity for youths and even older individuals to find satisfying work. It also allows you to obtain the experience of operating a relatively simple, small business, as well as realizing the fulfillment that comes with its success.

Chapter 2

GETTING JOBS

As long as grass grows, there will always be jobs. But in order to get the jobs, you will have to advertise. It's the only way to acquire customers. Advertising is absolutely essential in any type of service business.

For example, some service businesses such as those that do roofing, siding, and remodeling work, have to invest a considerable sum of money in advertising just to attract customers and get jobs. However, in the mowing business, there are several inexpensive methods of advertising. After you see how to get the jobs, you'll appreciate the fact that it can be done with very little money. What's mainly required, more than anything else, is your own initiative,

It all begins with you. You're the boss; this allows you to create your own unlimited opportunities. It's a chance to make more money and become more independent. Also, it can give you a great feeling.

The very first thing you've got to know to get started is how to find the jobs. There's more than one way to go about it. Advertising in a newspaper is one way. Knocking on people's doors is another way. And using business cards is a third way, the best way.

ADVERTISING

Let's consider newspaper advertising. Generally, advertising in a newspaper will bring only a few jobs. Besides, it can be expensive. You would have to run your ad many times. And each time the ad runs, you must pay the advertising cost which would cover the entire newspaper circulation. Consequently, you pay for advertising coverage that extends considerably out of town and far beyond your neighborhood. It's not worth it.

Furthermore, only a few of the people who live within your local area would see the ad and read it. In fact, many people don't read the newspaper.

You're much better off to concentrate your advertising efforts on an area that is within a reasonable distance from home. And you need to advertise in a more effective manner than using a newspaper. Essentially, it will be necessary to directly contact many of the people who live in your neighborhood. This leads to the consideration of knocking on doors and asking people if you can mow their lawns.

Knocking on doors is an effective way to advertise, but there are also drawbacks. Some people don't like to be disturbed, particularly if they happen to be talking on the telephone or watching their favorite TV program. You may irritate someone and end up losing a potential customer. Another drawback is that some of the people you ask "Can I mow your lawn?" feel confronted with having to give a direct "yes" or "no" answer. They resent it.

There is a more polite, businesslike approach to advertising without having to bother people in their homes. This is by using business cards. Business cards do the talking for you. They're small cards that state your name, address, telephone number, and the service that you're offering. The cards are delivered to homes throughout the neighborhood, without requiring an on-the-spot "yes" or "no" reply, and without disturbing anyone either. Using them will be the least expensive and most effective way to get jobs.

BUSINESS CARDS

Business cards can either be made by hand or by hiring a printer to do them professionally. It will cost about $40.00 to have them done by a printer. And, as a rule, it usually takes the printer at least a week because he's often so busy with other printing jobs. However, you can save time and money by printing them yourself. It takes about four hours, at most, to hand print 100 cards.

If you print them by hand, use index cards. Index cards are stiff, white cards with faint colored lines on them. The lines are helpful for printing neatly. They can be purchased in just about any department store or stationery store. Ask for the "three-inch by five-inch" size cards. A package of 100 cards costs about two dollars. One hundred should be sufficient to get you started.

Once you've obtained the cards and have begun to print, what should you say? Actually, very little. Business cards are used to communicate brief, simple messages.

Look at the sample business card shown in Figure 1. This sample can be used as a guide for making your own cards. Note that the word "reliable" is used. You should consider it to be an important word. People who want to hire someone to mow their lawn are looking for a reliable person to do it, someone they can depend upon.

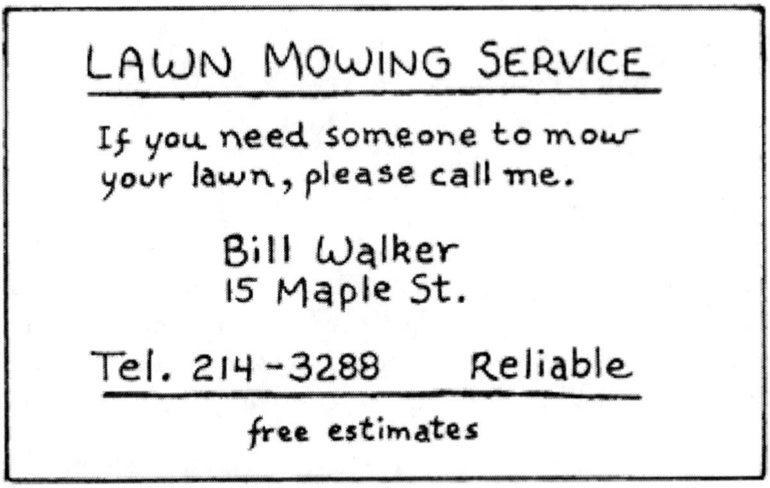

LAWN MOWING SERVICE

If you need someone to mow your lawn, please call me.

Bill Walker
15 Maple St.

Tel. 214-3288   Reliable

free estimates

FIGURE 1. *Sample Business Card*

Notice that the name of the town and state are omitted from the address. This is because the full address isn't necessary when advertising only within your local area.

There's a particular reason for stating "free estimates" on the business card. First of all, people who will consider hiring you expect you to estimate the size of the job and quote them a price. Secondly, they don't expect to pay for an estimate. So state that you're offering free estimates. This brings more calls. And just about everyone who calls will hire you. (There are various methods for doing quick estimates which are covered in the chapter on ESTIMATING.)

DISTRIBUTING BUSINESS CARDS

After the cards are printed, you're ready to advertise -- spread the word. Advertising is done by delivering the cards to certain groups of people. Actually, everyone who has to maintain a lawn is a prospect. But there are certain groups of people that will provide the majority of jobs. They consist of six prime marketing areas of interest for distributing the business cards.

The principal marketing areas are as follows:

- Real-Estate Brokers
- Landlords of Apartment Buildings
- Professional Businessmen
- Managers of Restaurants and Motels
- Lawn Mower Repairmen
- Homeowners

These are the prime markets for getting small lawn mowing jobs. Other types of markets which consist of golf courses, cemeteries, schools, parks, and the sides of roadways are all big jobs -- too big. They're strictly for experienced contractors with large, expensive mowing equipment.

You can distribute your business cards to any one, or all, of these prime marketing areas. However, the methods of delivering the cards are not the same for each group of people. Each group must be considered separately.

REAL-ESTATE BROKERS

Real-estate brokers are salesmen who specialize in the selling of land, homes, and businesses. As part of their normal routine of doing business, they advertise that a home is for sale by posting a "For Sale" sign on the property, usually on the front lawn. You've probably seen many of these signs. The broker's name and telephone number are on the sign. When you see one, give the real-estate broker a call and inquire if he/she may need your mowing services for that particular house or for any other properties which he/she is selling.

Sometimes the owner of a home will move away, leaving his/her house unoccupied, and a broker will assume responsibility for having the lawn mowed until the property has been sold. The broker usually is concerned about keeping the lawn neat in appearance so that the property always looks presentable to interested buyers; therefore, if you see a "For Sale" sign on the property of an unoccupied home and the grass is long overdue for cutting, this is a strong indication that the broker needs someone to mow the lawn. There's a good chance you'll be hired.

A real-estate broker will often own several properties as investments. These investment properties can provide more mowing jobs in addition to the properties that the broker is trying to sell for other people. For this reason alone, it's worth contacting all the local real-estate brokers. They're listed in the yellow pages of the telephone directory under "Real Estate".

When contacting brokers for mowing jobs, also ask them for the name and phone number of a real-estate agency that specializes in "relocation services". This is a particular type of real-estate agency that offers services which are specifically dedicated to taking care of the homes of absentee owners. Their services include hiring someone to mow the lawns. Most areas have an agency of this kind. All the other real-estate brokers in the area usually know who it is and are willing to inform you because you'll be offering a needed service.

So there are three good reasons to contact real-estate brokers. First, they may need your mowing services for one or more of the properties which they are selling for their clients. Second, they generally have several of their own properties for which they may need your mowing services. Third, they can perhaps tell you the name of a real-estate brokerage firm that specializes in relocation services, and this could lead to other mowing jobs.

LANDLORDS

Most areas have at least a few apartment buildings. There may even be many apartments where you live. The landlords who own these apartment buildings are responsible for the general maintenance of the property. Maintenance includes mowing the lawn. Some landlords, rather than cut the grass themselves, will hire someone to do it.

Therefore, contact the landlords of apartment buildings and give them your business card. Even if they don't need your services immediately, they might consider hiring you in the future.

Some landlords do not live in their own apartment building; and because of this, they can be difficult to reach, When this is the case, leave your card with one of the tenants. Ask a tenant to pass it along to the landlord the next time he/she pays the rent. Most tenants are friendly and willing to do this for you.

PROFESSIONAL BUSINESSMEN

Many doctors, lawyers, dentists, and bankers keep nice-looking, tidy lawns. Most of them never cut their own grass. They hire someone. You're probably already quite familiar with the locations of some of these professional businesses in your community. Nevertheless, look in the yellow pages of the telephone directory and record the names and addresses of all of them. This way you won't miss any.

Deliver your business cards directly to their business locations. The great majority of them will not need your services at the time you deliver the cards. There's a good chance that someone else is already doing the mowing work. But, whenever they need a replacement, they will have your card and know whom to call. It's just a matter of waiting.

Professional businessmen are often quite busy. So when you deliver the cards, more than likely, the secretaries will take them. This can be good because a professional businessman will often ask his secretary if she knows you or would recommend you. Her recommendation can carry a lot of weight. So try to make a good impression on the secretary. Introduce yourself and tell her that you mow lawns. Hand her your card and ask if she would save it for future consideration. She'll usually tell her boss that you were there, show him your card, and then save it.

MANAGERS OF RESTAURANTS AND MOTELS

If you live in an area that attracts tourists, there will probably be a lot of restaurants and motels. If not, then there are likely to be some restaurants and maybe a few motels. Check the yellow pages of the telephone directory to get a listing of all the motels and restaurants in your area.

Visit these places of business. Walk in and ask to speak with the manager. Keep the conversation brief. First, introduce yourself. Then tell the manager:

1. That you mow lawns.
2. That you would like to leave your business card.
3. And, to please give a call if you're needed.

If the manager accepts the card but appears to be in a hurry, just say "thank you" and leave. They're busy people and will respect you for respecting their time. Should the manager decide to talk with you, you may be getting a job quicker than you realized.

The lawn mowing markets which are associated with real estate brokers, landlords, professional businessmen, and managers of restaurants and motels may initially get you only a few customers. However, you'll get more calls for jobs later in the mowing season. These markets are easily and quickly covered, and you will be building the potential for future business.

MOWER REPAIRMAN

Many of the people that own a home suddenly find that they are unable to mow their lawn at one time or another. This happens because their mower won't operate properly and is therefore in need of repair. Like most people who are in this predicament, instead of buying a new mower, they will have the old one fixed. They take it to a lawn mower repairman. The repairman usually has to tell them it will be a few weeks before he can start working on it. The period for repair can often take two or three weeks because repairmen will frequently have a backlog of several other mowers in need of repair. This length of service period is not uncommon with lawn mower repairmen.

In the meantime, a person's lawn needs to be mowed, and they don't have a mower. What do they do? Well, probably for the first time in their life they may consider hiring someone to cut their grass. This isn't an unusual situation. It happens to various people throughout the mowing season.

Now back to the mower repairman. Suppose he were to ask his customers if they would be interested in taking a business card of someone who would mow their lawn until the mower was fixed. Any of his customers that would be interested would take the card and know whom to call. Therefore, the repairman continually comes in direct contact with people who are in need of having interim mowing services while their mowers are in the process of being repaired. He can hand out your business cards to some of his customers. This is why you should visit mower repairmen and offer to leave some of your cards with them. Check the yellow pages of your telephone directory either under "Lawn Mower Engines", "Engines – Gasoline," or "Lawn Mowers" to ensure that you find all the local mower repairmen.

When you talk to a repairman and suggest leaving some of your business cards with him, he'll be glad you came. You can relieve some of the pressure from his tight schedule of trying to repair mowers in a hurry.

The cards will provide him with an alternative by enabling him to offer your temporary mowing services to his customers.

Chances are good that when one of his customers takes your card, they will give you a call. Even though these would be temporary customers, they can sometimes turn out to be regular customers. Some people, after hiring someone to mow their lawn, appreciate the convenience of the service and allow it to continue.

Jobs tend to come relatively slow from business cards which are left with a repairman. However, these cards will be effective for getting occasional jobs all through the mowing season. And the number of jobs that are able to be acquired, when considered over an entire mowing season, can be quite significant. To go after the jobs in this market, you must have a mower.

There's another way in which mower repairmen can be of assistance. If you talk to one who has a relatively small lawn, you may consider offering to cut his grass in exchange for free, quick repair work in the event that your mower should need repairs. This type of an offer was made to a repairman, and he accepted. Even if you don't make such an offer, most repairmen will usually give you immediate repair services once they know you're in the mowing business. They realize you need the mower soon to continue conducting your business.

HOMEOWNERS

As the name implies, these are the people who own homes. The homeowner market is where you'll find the most mowing jobs. It's the biggest market available. Homeowners provide the best and quickest response for jobs in a short period of time. They also have a tendency to be the best-paying customers. Concentrate heavily on the homeowner market. This is where you should distribute the majority of your business cards.

One of the ways that a business card can be delivered to a homeowner is by putting the card inside of a newspaper that will be delivered to his home. To do this, you will need to have a newspaper carrier help you. If a newspaper carrier agrees to help, then this is what you do.

Offer to go along with the carrier while newspaper deliveries are being made. Each time a delivery is to be made to a rather nice looking home, which appears as if the homeowner can afford to hire you, put your business card inside of the newspaper. Insert it deep inside, immediately behind the front page. Any home that appears as if the grass is long overdue for cutting is also a prime candidate home for a mowing job.

This is an easy, polite way to get business cards into some of the best homes without disturbing anyone. While reading the newspaper in a relaxed state of mind, the homeowners will see your card and read it. This is also when they'll take time to give it serious consideration. Generally, homeowners will do any one of three things after reading the cards:

1. Call you because they're interested in hiring someone.
2. Save the card because they might become interested in hiring someone and, if so, they will know who to call.
3. Throw the card away because they're definitely not interested.

As a rule, you won't receive any calls the same day that the cards are delivered. It takes time before a homeowner will decide to call. However, most people who are interested will call you within two weeks.

Using the newspaper method is one way of distributing the cards. This method is suggested because it works. But you have a choice. There is another method which works just as well and sometimes better:

You can choose to deliver your cards to homes by attaching them to the front door as shown in Figure 2. With this method, you attach your business card about two feet above the doorknob, where clearly visible at eye level. Use a piece of masking tape to hold the card in place. Masking tape is sticky enough to firmly attach the card, but not sticky enough to pull off any paint when a homeowner removes it. It's also easily removed from the business card.

You don't have to knock on the door. Just leave the card. Should someone unexpectedly come to the door, hand them the card. Explain that you're distributing business cards and looking for jobs to mow lawns. You may even inquire whether the person knows someone else who might be interested in hiring you. Some people are well informed and can advise you accordingly --perhaps lead you directly to a job.

BUSINESS CARD
MASKING TAPE

FIGURE 2. *Distribution of Business Cards to Homeowners*

Very few people come to the door. So the cards can be distributed about as fast as you're able to walk from one home to another. It doesn't take much time. A large area of your neighborhood can be covered in a single day. Incidentally, it's not only the people who live in the nicest homes that can afford to hire you. But if you select a lot of these types of homes at first, it should give you some advantage when getting started.

Homeowners respond to the business cards quite well. However, they respond best of all just before the mowing season begins. Occasionally, a few of the homeowners will even make some complimentary remarks to you such as "I liked your business card." "You're going places," or "I felt that anyone who would take time to distribute a business card would also be reliable and do a good job."

FIGURE 3. *On the Job*

MAILBOXES

Resist the temptation to distribute business cards by putting them inside of mailboxes. This may seem like a good idea, but it's illegal - a federal offense. To open someone's mailbox is a violation of the privacy of that person's mail. Therefore, as a solid rule:

DO NOT OPEN ANYONE'S MAILBOX!!

Here's an example of what can happen. There were some boys in Ohio who were getting started in the lawn mowing business during the summer of 1982. They had innocently distributed their advertising flyers, or circulars, by putting them inside mailboxes. One particular homeowner became angry and reported them for doing this. As a result, they had to pay a fine which was significant enough to put them out of business. It is a very serious offense, at any age.

SHOPPING GUIDE

Originally, it was mentioned that a newspaper would not be very effective for advertising and that it would be too expensive. This is true as a general rule. However, you may consider advertising in a small, local, weekly circular (as opposed to a large, daily newspaper) if the publication has a lot of advertising. These circulars are commonly referred to as "shopping guides". They typically contain a significant amount of local advertising and are therefore read more as a shopping guide rather than for news. People browse through them to see what products and services are available.

A shopping guide can be effective for getting customers, and the advertising cost is usually inexpensive. You could try running an ad only a few times to see how well it does. It's not very probable that the ad would do as well as the business cards. The cards have been found to be the best means of advertising. But if you were to distribute business cards and also advertise in a shopping guide, this would be the fastest way of all to get jobs.

Here's an example of a simple, effective ad that has been used to produce enough customers to be worth the investment in advertising. Assume your name is John Anderson, you live in a town called Lakeville, and your telephone number is 223-4828. This is how the ad would read if you did not have a mower:

> LAWN MOWING SERVICE
> Covering Lakeville area.
> Free estimates. Reliable.
> John Anderson, 223-4828

This is how the ad would read if you did have a mower:

> LAWN MOTING SERVICE
> Covering Lakeville area.
> Free estimates. Reliable.
> Mower provided.
> John Anderson, 223-4828

MARKET ASSESSMENTS

Advertising with business cards is a proven method. It's inexpensive, easy, and it works. Obviously, the more cards you distribute, the more jobs you will get. The markets which include real-estate brokers, landlords, professional businessmen, and managers of restaurants and motels, will all have about the same advertising response. The initial response, during the first month, should bring somewhere between three and eight customers for every 100 cards distributed. As the season continues, there should be at least a few more responses.

Responses from a mower repairman are about two to five calls per month, depending on the repairman's business volume. Homeowners will bring somewhere between four and 12 customers per 100 cards distributed. An ad in a shopping guide, with a circulation of 5,000 copies, will bring about three customers per month. These market assessments are made on the basis of three years of advertising experience. See Figure 4 for a summary of marketing assessments.

To further evaluate the business card method, it was also tested in two different, remote communities by others who were interested in mowing lawns. In one case there were two boys nearing the end of their junior year of high school. They formed a partnership. One of them had an old pick-up truck, and both had the use of their parents' lawn mowers. They distributed 450 cards in their small town of 3,000 people and got 35 customers within two weeks. This was nearly an 8% response. Two years later they were still mowing lawns. Their business had grown to the point where both of them were earning their way through college.

In another case, a senior high school student who had the use of his father's mower and no means of transportation other than walking, limited his coverage to within walking distances. He lived far out in the country near a lake where he was able to distribute business cards. The cards were distributed mainly to lakeside cottages. Within one week he had eight customers.

MARKET	GENERAL ASSESSMENT	RESPONSE
REAL-ESTATE BROKERS	Only a few customers will come from ordinary brokers. But, brokers who specialize in handling "relocation services" can potentially provide many customers.	These four markets will initially provide from three to eight customers for every 100 cards distributed. A few more customer calls will come as the season continues.
LANDLORDS	Landlords of small apartment dwellings with between two and 10 units are a fair market for getting customers. Large apartment complexes are more difficult to get, and the landlords of these buildings don't pay as well.	
PROFESSIONAL BUSINESSMEN	This market will initially provide only a few customers. But, over the long run, the response will improve. It's a slow responding market that takes time to penetrate.	
MANAGERS OF RESTAURANTS AND MOTELS	This market will initially provide only a few customers. But, over the long run, the response will improve. This also is a slow responding market that takes time to penetrate.	
MOWER REPAIRMEN	Repairmen will provide a rather slow but steady flow of temporary customers all through the mowing season. About one-third of these customers will hire you to mow their lawns on a regular basis.	About two to five jobs per month, depending on a repairman's work load.
HOMEOWNERS	This is the best market of all. Concentrate heavily on homeowners. They provide a quick response. It's the easiest market to penetrate.	About four to 12 customers for every 100 cards distributed.
SHOPPING GUIDE	Advertising in a shopping guide reaches all markets simultaneously. This can be another effective means of advertising, along with the business cards.	About three customers per month for every 5,000 people of advertising coverage.

In all cases, customer responses are best at the beginning of the mowing season.

FIGURE 4. *Marketing Assessments*

This was an exceptional response of 16%. The boy had attributed his outstanding results to the fact that a lot of people who own lakeside cottages often live at their homes during the week and stay at their cottages on the weekend. And instead of having to mow two lawns, transporting their mower back and forth between home and cottage, these people would rather hire someone to mow the cottage lawn. Another possible reason is that people like to relax while at their cottage and therefore don't want to have to be concerned about mowing the lawn.

The majority of customers that you acquire during a mowing season will automatically continue with your mowing services the following season. Just give them a call at the beginning of the next season so they will know that you're still in business.

CHAPTER 3

EXAMPLES

O ne way of getting a feeling for doing something without having had any experience is by seeing examples. Therefore, there are examples of lawn mowing jobs included in the back section of this chapter (Figures 7 through 17). The examples are presented by showing the properties of many customers, along with essential statistics and comments. Each property represents an actual customer during the spring, summer, and fall seasons of 1980 and 1981, which were baseline years for collecting all the original data.

The location is in a hilly section of Berkshire County, Massachusetts, in a small mill-town with a population of 6,300 people. Levels of income and levels of employment in the town were running close to the United States' national average. Although 1981 was a year of deepening recession, it did not seem to affect the mowing business. People still spent money to have their lawns mowed on a regular basis. And they paid just as generously in 1981 as they did in 1980. Payments which were received from the customers are given in the examples, in 1981 dollars. (Updated prices are given in Chapter 4.)

A wide range of various sized properties are included in the examples. They range in size from 0.12 acres (requiring 15 minutes of mowing time) to 0.37 acres (requiring nearly 2 1/2 hours of mowing time). Each example shows: the property outline and dimensions; the size of the house lot; mowing time; payment; hourly rate of pay; degree of slopes; whether or not the customer provided a lawn mower; and, what the job consisted of (mowing, trimming, raking).

The customers are not identified by their real names. Instead, each customer is given a code-name to protect their privacy. They are identified as Mr. "A", Mr. "B", Mrs. "C", Mrs. "D", Mrs. "E", Mr. "F", Mrs. "G", Mrs. "H", Mrs. "I", Mrs. "J", and Mr. "K". Their properties are shown in increasing order of the sizes of the house lots, starting with the property of Mr. "A" (which is the smallest house lot) and ending with the property of Mr. "K" (which is the largest house lot). Each house lot is drawn to the same scale so that the relative sizes of the lots can be compared. So if any particular house lot appears to be about twice the size of another, then it really is.

PROPERTY OUTLINES

The outline of each property is shown from a "bird's-eye" view, as would be seen from high above. Shown are the outlines of the property, the house, driveway, walkway, stone walls, bushes, hedges, and the street in front of the property. Shaded areas indicate where there is grass, showing the amount of lawn to be mowed.

Trees have been omitted. This was done to keep the drawings of the house lots as simple and clear-looking as possible.

PROPERTY DIMENSIONS

The dimensions of each property are given in feet. These dimensions were determined by pacing the property lines while mowing, and then converting the number of paces to the length in feet. Measuring distances by using the pacing method is a way of determining the true surface length of the land. It gives a fairly accurate length of the lawn going over mounds and slopes.

Distances measured and recorded by a registered land surveyor do not account for slopes, bankings, and irregularities in the terrain. Surveyors measure only horizontal distance, as though the land were perfectly level. It is required of them by law, but it gives a smaller surface area than what really exists on a parcel of land. Therefore, the pacing method gives a more accurate representation for the purposes of considering a surface area of land to be mowed.

Being able to see the dimensions of the house lots serves as an aid in visualizing the lengths and widths of the properties. Furthermore, it was necessary to know the dimensions for the purpose of calculating the land area, or lot size, of the properties.

SIZE OF HOUSE LOTS

The size of each house lot is given in acres, which is the standard unit of measure of an area of land. An acre is a sizable piece of property. It contains 43,560 square feet of land, which would be equivalent to a square area of about 209 feet by 209 feet. A football field is about 1.1 acres, considerably larger than the average house lot.

None of the properties in the examples consist of a full acre of land. The smallest lot, with 0.12 acres, is slightly more than one-tenth the size of a football field. The largest lot, with 0.37 acres, is one-third the size of a football field. This is why you will see that all the house lots have only a fraction of an acre of land. And the amount of lawn to be mowed is even less because of the space occupied by the house, driveway, and walk ways.

MOWING TIME

The amount of mowing time for each property is stated in the examples. An average time over several mowings is given. Therefore, the mowing time for various sizes of house lots can be compared. Mowing time can be tricky. For example, most people would think it takes about half as much time to mow a lot that is half the size of another lot. But actually, it takes less than half the time. This can best be understood by making comparisons with the property of Mr. "A" and the property of Mrs. "E". Mr. "A's" lot size is 0.12 acres, exactly half the size of Mrs. "E's", which is 0.24 acres. Yet the mowing time for Mr. "A's" property is only 15 minutes compared with one hour to do Mrs. "E's" property. Therefore, Mr. "A's" property can be mowed in just one-fourth the amount of time that it takes to mow Mrs. "E's" property. Why? Because Mr. "A" has only one-fourth the amount of lawn as Mrs. "E". His lot size is so small that the house, driveways and walk way occupy about half of his property space.

If both of these properties were 100% lawn -- vacant lots, completely covered with grass -- then, under these special conditions, it would, indeed take about half as much time to mow Mr. "A's" lot as it would take to mow Mrs. "E's" lot. When lot sizes get to be larger than one-third of an acre, the mowing time then begins to increase more directly in proportion to the size of the lot. One-third of an acre is the point at which the land area covered by a house, driveway, and walkway becomes relatively insignificant in comparison to the size of the lot.

Mowing time can vary, depending upon the length and thickness of grass and the size of the mower being used. The jobs illustrated in the examples were done with a 20-inch-wide, three-horsepower, rotary mower, which was pushed by hand (not self-propelled). This type of mower (shown in Figure 5) was used because it is relatively inexpensive, reasonably fast-cutting, and easily maneuvered into most tight spaces (without having to do any trimming). Also, it's not heavy. A considerable amount of grass can be cut without tiring.

PAYMENTS: MORE FOR LESS

The payments received show a surprising trend. In the lawn mowing business, customers are willing to pay more for less. They are willing to pay considerably more money, on an hourly basis, for small lots than for large lots. Most profitable are those lots which are smaller than one-quarter of an acre. And these require only one hour, or less, of mowing time.

HOURLY RATES OF PAY

A person's hourly rate of pay, which is often referred to as just "hourly rate", is the amount of money earned in an hour, it's a measure of the value of one's time. The hourly rates of pay for mowing lawns are not the same for every house lot. It varies significantly for different sizes of lots.

Hourly rates of pay have been calculated and given in each example so that the rates for different sizes of house lots can be compared. The hourly rates were determined as a result of dividing the payment received by the mowing time. Thus, if a payment of 10 dollars was received for mowing a lot that required one hour of mowing time, then 10 dollars divided by one hour is a rate of pay of 10 dollars an hour.

Ten dollars an hour was easily an average hourly rate for mowing small lots of less than one-quarter of an acre. For instance, consider the five smallest house lots shown in the examples. These are the properties of Mr. "A", Mr. "B", Mrs. "C", Mrs. "D", and Mrs. "E". The average hourly rate for these customers was $12 and hour. This is quite considerable. In fact, by comparison, the average hourly earnings of non-farm workers in the Untied States at this same time (summer of 1981) was $7.19 per hour.

Most customers are willing to pay a fixed sum of money to have their lawns mowed, without consideration of what it cost them on an hourly basis. This is especially true for small lots.

This is the mower that was used. It's a three-horsepower, 20-inch, self-push rotary mower; This kind of mower is highly recommended over the self-driven type or riding type of mowers for small lawns. It has many advantages. Being relatively lightweight, it's easy to oper-ate and maneuver and easy to transport between jobs. The simple construction offers a minimal amount of mechanical parts that are subject to failure; It's also one of the least expensive mowers.

FIGURE 5. *Recommended Mower*

SLOPES OF HOUSE LOTS

With each example there is a brief statement about the slope of the lot, stating whether the lot is level, on a slight slope, or on a medium slope. Steep slopes are not mentioned. This is because none of the example house lots are situated on steep slopes.

A lot classified as being "level" is really only approximately level, in that it has no incline of greater than a five-degree angle. A lot that is classified as being "slightly sloped" has an average incline somewhere between five and 10 degrees of angle. And a lot that is classified as being on a "medium slope" has an incline somewhere between 10 and 20 degrees of angle. Any lot with an average incline exceeding 20 degrees of angle is considered to be "steep".

See Figure 6 for degrees of slopes.

Most of the house lots in the examples are classified as being "level".

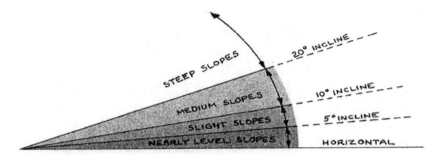

FIGURE 6. *Degrees of Slopes*

The great majority of properties are landscaped to eliminate having steep slopes. Most are either level, on a slight slope, or on a medium slope. Those which are on a slight slope have only little effect on increasing the mowing time (beyond what would be required if these same lots were level). Those which are on a medium slope have somewhat more effect on increasing the mowing time. However, a lot situated on a hill, or a long steep slope, can have significant effect on increasing the mowing time, particularly if the average incline exceeds 25 degrees or more.

As a rule, it's best to avoid the steep-sloped jobs. These types of house lots require relentless physical energy to mow. They are exhausting, and a customer usually doesn't want to pay due compensation for the extra effort. After mowing just one of these lots, there is a natural tendency to avoid them thereafter. There are enough mowing jobs without having to accept one with a steep slope. Typically, only a very small percentage of the homes are situated on steep slopes.

REASONS FOR BEING HIRED

The various reasons that a customer will hire you are interesting; some just don't have the time to mow their own lawn. Others have time, but would rather hire someone than mow it themselves. Then there are those who are in poor health, and therefore physically unable to do their own mowing work. These are people afflicted with conditions such as arthritis, heart trouble, breathing problems, or poor blood circulation.

Another group consists of people who ordinarily do their own mowing, but, because they either need to buy a new lawn mower or have the old one repaired, they will hire someone. Consequently, they may decide to rehire the same person for a long time thereafter (as a result of appreciating the convenience of having someone else mow the lawn). Yet another reason for being hired is that a particular individual who used to mow a person's lawn is no longer available to perform the service any more -- the boy who did it previously went away to college or the man who did it previously has retired.

In all cases, when you're hired, the customer likes to feel that you can be trusted on the property and that you will be reliable enough to come and mow the lawn with some reasonable degree of regularity. Getting the lawn mowed within one or two days after a customer asks you to mow it is often considered as being sufficiently reliable.

The customers paid quite regularly. Most paid in cash. A few paid by check.

There were no unpaid debts.

TYPES OF WORK

There are three closely related types of work which would appear to be equally in demand in the lawn mowing business: mowing, trimming, and raking. One would tend to think that trimming a lawn after mowing it, and then also raking the fresh clippings, would be normal routines involved in the mowing business. But this was not the case. It was discovered that most customers were mainly interested in mowing only. There's generally very little concern about trimming (which is understandable when you realize how close a mower can get to the edges of a house, fence, bushes, walls, and so on). There also wasn't much concern about raking the fresh clippings. Consequently, this is why you will see a statement in

10 of the 11 examples saying that the "job consisted of mowing only". It means that no trimming and no raking was included in the work.

In just one of the examples the job consisted of some raking work. This particular customer, Mrs. "G", wanted the leaves raked once a year, in the fall. But she never requested that the grass clippings be raked during the mowing season. In fact, none of the customers ever requested that their grass be raked after it was mowed.

Most people give their lawn a good raking twice a year, usually in the early spring and again in the fall. Apparently, this is enough annual raking without having to rake the freshly mowed grass clippings during the mowing season. Actually, it makes sense not to rake all the grass clippings.

Clippings decompose to form decayed vegetation. This is food for night crawlers, causing them to burrow to the surface and feed during late evening hours. The many tiny tunnels made by the crawlers allow free nitrogen in the air to come in direct contact with grass roots, fertilizing the lawn. Additionally, the excrement, or waste matter, left behind by the crawlers is also a fertilizer; it gets spread by rain, further enriching the soil.

There are two exceptions to when grass clippings should be raked. One is if a lawn has been neglected to the extent that the grass has grown quite tall. After mowing a lawn in this condition, the clippings lie around in thick, heavy clumps, flattening down the lawn in spotty areas, cutting off sunlight and fresh air supply. These areas get smothered, killing the grass.

The other exception applies to certain locations where there are no night crawlers. These locations are mainly in the southern half of the United States. Wherever there are no night crawlers, there is a greater need to rake the clippings.

If ever a customer should want the clippings raked after each mowing, it's best to invest in a bag that can be attached to the mower and catch the clippings at the same time you're mowing. And should any customer want trimming done, it's best to buy a small, powered, spinning-string type of trimmer. They're easy to use and very fast cutting. Trimming with hand clippers is absolutely too time-consuming.

A "side benefit" in the lawn mowing business is that occasionally odd jobs will be offered to you. These jobs can consist of weeding gardens, clipping hedges, planting small trees, washing windows, and painting fences, as examples, There's nothing wrong with accepting the odd jobs if you have time and need money. But customers do not pay as well for odd jobs as they do for mowing services. Your greatest profits, by far, will come from specializing in mowing.

YOUR OWN MOWER

Each example has a brief statement saying whether or not the customer provided a lawn mower. Only four of the 11 customers provided one. So, you can see that by having your own mower, there is a good chance of easily doubling, and almost tripling, the number of your customers.

There is another advantage to having your own mower. Customers feel they should pay you more money. They understand that there is an investment in the mower and that, occasionally, it requires maintenance. They also understand that you are providing the gasoline and oil to operate it (even though this amounted to only about 22 cents per mowing).

The inexpensive mower used in the examples went through two six-month mowing seasons with relatively little professional maintenance required. It was serviced just once, for $20, requiring carburetor repair and replacement of the starting- switch assembly.

The mower had been purchased new, on sale, for $88. Hence, the cost for the mower had amounted to $88, plus the $20 for maintenance, or $108, total. Gasoline (and oil) for operating costs were about $56. Therefore, the overall expenses for the mower, its maintenance, and its operation for two mowing seasons was $108 plus $56, for a sum of $164.

There were also expenses for advertising. It had cost approximately $1 for 100 index cards which were used for hand-printing business cards that were delivered to homes. Also, an ad had been placed twice in a small, local, weekly "shopping guide". The two ads were almost $4 each, which came to nearly $8. Therefore, the total advertising cost was about $9.

Incidentally, the $1 spent for making business cards had produced more customers than the $8 for advertising in the local shopping guide. The expenses are summarized as follows:

Mower Cost	$ 88
Maintenance Cost	$ 20
Operating Cost	$ 56
Advertising Cost	$ 9
Total Expenses	$ 173 (1981 dollars)

These are the total expenses (in 1981 dollars) that had been accumulated over two mowing seasons while mowing lawns for 11 customers. The price of a new, three-horsepower, 20-inch, self-push rotary mower, in 2007, is about $300.

INCOME

There was a total income of $2,386 earned over the two-season period. After subtracting the $173 of expenses, there was $2,213 in clear profit. This is the amount of profit that had been earned in 320 hours of mowing time (160 hours during each mowing season). It's equivalent to having worked only four, 40-hour weeks during each of the two six-month mowing seasons. The working hours, on a weekly basis, were an average of just six hours and 10 minutes. Not very demanding. Working on a regular, full-time schedule (at 40 hours a week) would have produced an income of approximately $300 each week, and for 52 consecutive weeks, this would reflect an annual income rate of $15,600 per year (in 1981 dollars).

Obviously, the income would have been more for more than 11 customers. During John's fifth mowing season (1984) he had 50 customers and was earning nearly $1,000 a week. (More details are given in the EPILOGUE) And considering that 11 customers had required only a little more than six hours a week of mowing time, there was significant room for growth of income. Therefore, it's just a matter of how much available free time you have and how ambitious you are. Also, depending upon where you live, if the mowing season is longer than a six-month period, this too would reflect an increase in income. There would be more mowings for each customer during the longer mowing season.

Something else that can affect the amount of income is the average size of the house lots of your customers. The income of $2,386 is what was earned from the 11 example customers with house lots that ranged from 0.12 acres (15 minutes of mowing time) to 0.37 acres (nearly 2 1/2 hours of mowing time). If all of the 11 examples were to have had house lots of less than 0.25 acres (requiring an hour, or less, of mowing time), where the average rate of pay, you will recall, had been $12 an hour, then the income would have been much greater than $2,386. The income, instead, would have been $3,840, about 60% more earnings. So, always try to get the smallest lawns.

Earning $12 an hour on a full-time basis would provide an income of $480 per 40-hour work week, and over 52 consecutive weeks; this would reflect an annual income rate of $24,960 a year. Mowing lawns can be lucrative, and it's a cash business. You can always make green from green by mowing lawns for money.*

*All of this income data was established in 1981, and therefore, it has been expressed in 1981 dollars. Prices in later-year dollars are significantly higher and are covered in Chapter 4, ESTIMATING.

STATISTICS

- Lot Size   0.12 Acres
- Mowing Time   15 Minutes
- Payment $3.00 (1981 dollars)
- Hourly Rate $12.00 Per Hour (1981 rate)

COMMENTS

- Level Property
- Customer Provided a Mower
- Job Consisted of Mowing Only

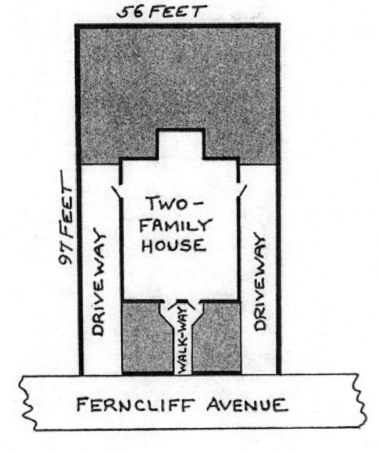

FIGURE 7. *Property of Mr. "A"*

STATISTICS

- Lot Size   0.16 Acres
- Mowing Time   30 Minutes
- Payment $6.00 (1981 dollars)
- Hourly Rate $12.00 Per Hour (1981 rate)

COMMENTS

- Level Property, Except For Small Banking Along One Side
- Customer Did Not Provide a Mower
- Job Consisted of Mowing Only

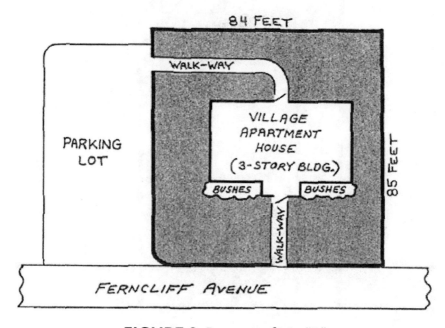

FIGURE 8. Property of Mr. "B"

STATISTICS

- Lot Size   0.17 Acres
- Mowing Time   30 Minutes
- Payment $7.00 (1981 dollars)
- Hourly Rate $14.00 Per hour (1981 rate)

COMMENTS

- Level Property
- Customer Provided a Mower
- Job Consisted of Mowing Only

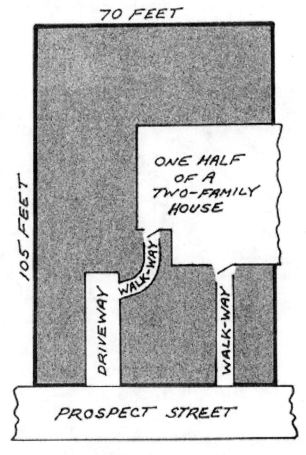

FIGURE 9. *Property of Mrs. "C"*

STATISTICS

- Lot Size   0.18 Acres
- Mowing Time   35 Minutes
- Payment $7.00 (1981 dollars)
- Hourly Rate $12.00 Per hour (1981 rate)

COMMENTS

- Level property except for slight slope along back yard
- Customer did not provide a mower
- Job consisted of mowing only

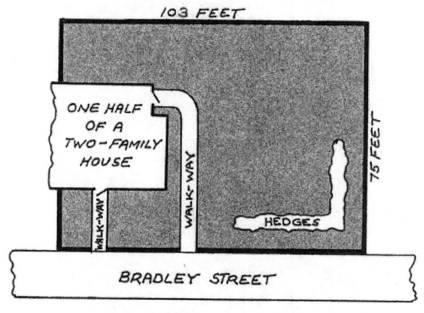

FIGURE 10. *Property of Mrs. "D"*

STATISTICS

- Lot Size   0.24 Acres
- Mowing Time   1 Hour
- Payment $10.00 (1981 dollars)
- Hourly Rate $10.00 Per hour (1981 rate)

COMMENTS

- Level property
- Customer provided a mower
- Job consisted of mowing only

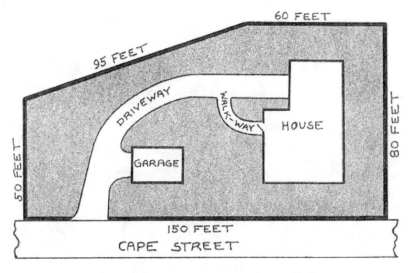

FIGURE 11. *Property of Mrs. "E"*

STATISTICS

- Lot Size   0.25 Acres
- Mowing Time   1 Hour
- Payment $8.00 (1981 dollars)
- Hourly Rate $8.00 Per hour (1981 rate)

COMMENTS

- Level property
- Customer did not provide a mower
- Job consisted of mowing only

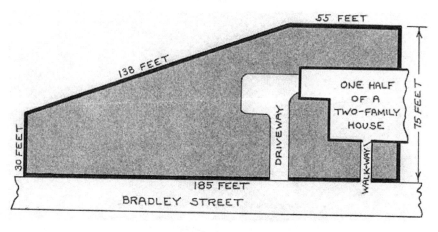

FIGURE 12. *Property of Mr. "F"*

STATISTICS

- Lot Size   0.26 Acres
- Mowing Time   1 Hour and 10 Minutes
- Payment $10.00 (1981 dollars)
- Hourly Rate $8.57 per hour (1981 rate)

COMMENTS

- Slightly sloped property with a short, steep banking along one side
- Customer did not provide a mower
- Job consisted of mowing only, except for raking leaves in the fall

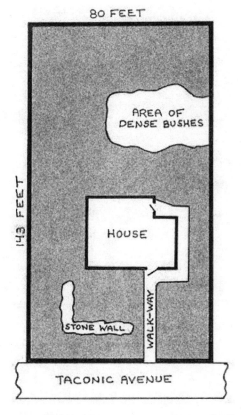

FIGURE 13. *Property of Mrs. "G"*

STATISTICS

- Lot Size   0.31 Acres
- Mowing Time   1 Hour and 40 Minutes
- Payment $10.00 (1981 dollars)
- Hourly Rate $6.00 per hour (1981 rate)

COMMENTS

- Level on half of the property; the other half is on a medium slope
- Customer did not provide a mower
- Job consisted of mowing only

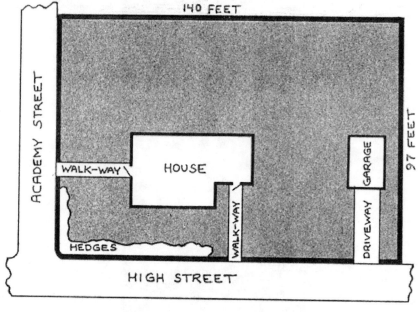

FIGURE 14. *Property of Mrs. "H"*

STATISTICS

- Lot Size   0.33 Acres
- Mowing Time   1 Hour and 50 Minutes
- Payment $10.00 (1981 dollars)
- Hourly Rate $5.46 per hour (1981 rate)

COMMENTS

- Level property
- Customer did not provide a mower
- Job consisted of mowing only

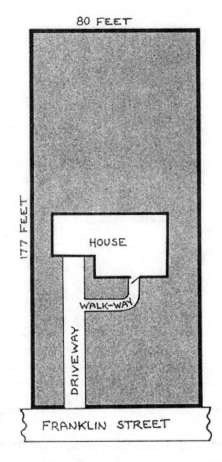

FIGURE 15. *Property of Mrs. "I"*

STATISTICS

- Lot Size   0.34 Acres
- Mowing Time   2 Hours
- Payment $10.00 (1981 dollars)
- Hourly Rate $5.00 per hour (1981 rate)

COMMENTS

- Level property
- Customer did not provide a mower
- Job consisted of mowing only

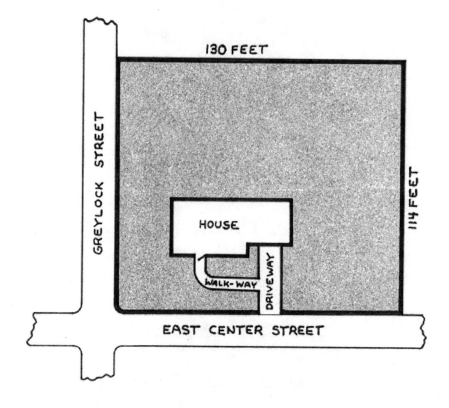

FIGURE 16. *Property of Mrs. "J"*

STATISTICS

- Lot Size   0.37 Acres
- Mowing Time   2 Hours and 25 Minutes
- Payment $15.00 (1981 dollars)
- Hourly Rate $6.21 per hour (1981 rate)

COMMENTS

- Slight slope along the entire property
- Customer provided the mower
- Job consisted of mowing only

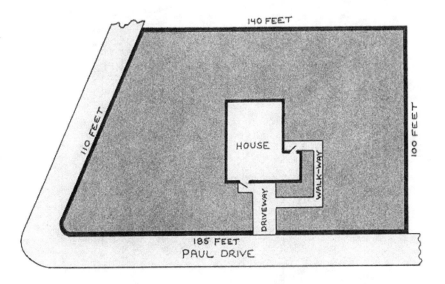

FIGURE 17. *Property of Mr. "K"*

Getting paid

CHAPTER 4

ESTIMATING

There are many types of businesses that perform different kinds of services for their customers. And they all have a system, or method, to determine the cost of doing work. The process of determining the cost is referred to as "estimating". It's an important part of a business.

Probably just about every person who is in business would prefer to charge their customers as much money as possible and earn maximum profits. However, the customers would prefer to pay as small a fee as possible and minimize their expenses. So, somewhere between these two extremes there is a price range where both parties will agree to an acceptable fee. The skill of good estimating is to be able to determine profitable prices that are within the acceptable range. With a little knowledge, anyone can do it.

By the time you're finished with this chapter, you'll have all the information you need -- enough to become an expert.

Although estimating can involve complicated procedures in most businesses, it can be reduced to a very simple method in the mowing business.

But first, we'll take a look at some already established prices and see the trends of how prices change from one size of house lot to another. We'll also look at other kinds of statistical data. After seeing the data, it will then be used to provide you with good, solid information for estimating.

STATISTICAL DATA

Lawn mowing data was collected as a result of actual experience with the 11 customers that were shown in the examples. This data has been compiled and arranged in such a way that, at a glance, you'll be able to observe the special considerations for estimating. The data is illustrated on certain charts, called "bar charts". There are three of these charts and each one of them will eventually be discussed in detail.

For the moment, they are mentioned and discussed only briefly. The first chart will show you how much time it takes to mow various sizes of house lots. This is the MOWING TIME bar chart (Figure 18). The second chart will show you how the payments, or prices, vary for different sizes of house lots. This is the PAYMENTS bar chart (Figure 21). The third chart will show you how the hourly rates of pay change for each size of house lot. This is the HOURLY RATES OF PAY bar chart (Figure 22). In each case, the mowing times, payments, and hourly rates of pay all depend on the size of a house lot. Therefore, by knowing only the size of a lot -- that's all -- you know enough information to determine a price for mowing. This is one way to set prices: set them according to the size of a house lot.

Another way to set prices is to set them based on the mowing time. Both ways work equally well because the size of a lot dictates the amount of mowing time required. Lot size and mowing time are interrelated -- the larger the lot, the longer the mowing time. Consequently, it's possible to determine a price either by knowing the size of a lot, or else by knowing the mowing time.

MOWING TIME

Assume that one of your prospective customers were to tell you the acreage of their house lot. As soon as you know the acreage, it's easy to readily determine how much time it will take to mow the lot. The duration of time required to mow various sizes of lots is shown in the MOWING TIME bar chart (Figure 18). The chart gives the interrelationship between lot size and mowing time.

The mowing times are based on using a 20-inch lawn mower, which is a common size mower. A smaller, 18-inch mower would require about 10% more mowing time. And a larger, 22-inch mower would require about 10% less mowing time.

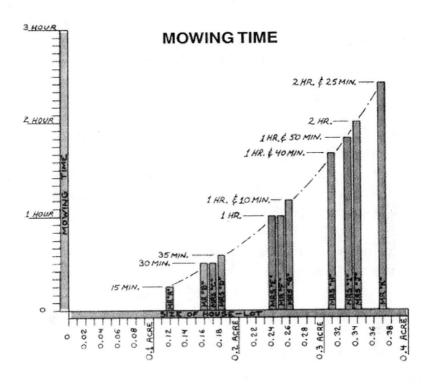

The bar chart shows the mowing time for various sizes of house lots. Each bar's vertical height represents the time to mow the different sized house lots of Mr. "A", Mr. "B", Mrs. "C", Mrs. "D", Mrs. "E", Mr. "F", Mrs. "G", Mrs. "H", Mrs. "I", Mrs. "J" and Mr. "K". Drawn along the top sections of the bars is a curved line that shows the mowing time for all lot sizes, from 0.12 to 0.37 acres. These mowing times are the average time that would be required, using a 20-inch mower.

Mowing time, for a given lot size, is quite predictable.

FIGURE 18. Mowing Time Bar Chart

While the MOWING TIME bar chart shows the relationship between lot size and mowing time, the chart could be somewhat difficult to use directly as an estimating aid. Therefore, the same information that is given in the chart is also given in the MOWING TIME ESTIMATING TABLE (Table 1), but in a more easily readable form. More important, though, the table includes an additional element of information: it has a column that gives the dimensions of a lot, in feet, which corresponds with the acreage. This information can be convenient for relating the dimensions of a lot (in feet) to the size of a lot (in acres). It is useful if you should want to pace the length and width of a house lot to determine the dimensions, and then find the corresponding acreage (or mowing time) in the table. Yet, this will seldom be necessary.

Most often, customers know, and can tell you, either the size of their lot or the mowing time. After they inform you, then quote them a price. But, of course, you can't quote prices until you know how much to charge. Nor can you estimate the size of lot until you know how it's done. This is where an understanding of estimating becomes helpful.

Estimating is accomplished in two basic steps. Step one involves determining either the size of a lot or the mowing time. Step two is to be able to quote a price based on either the lot size or the mowing time. Step one is discussed first.

ESTIMATING, STEP ONE

There are different methods that can be used to estimate the size of a lot or the mowing time. These methods include:

1. Simply "ask the customer".
2. Pace the lot to determine its dimensions and apply what's called the "equivalent square" method.
3. Find the lot size in a special look-up matrix, which is referred to as the "acreage matrix" method; and
4. Calculate the lot size using an "acreage equation" method.

TABLE I.
MOWING TIME ESTIMATING TABLE

SIZE OF HOUSE LOT		MOWING TIME
AREA	DIMENSIONS (IF THE LOT WERE SQUARE)	
0.12 ACRES	72 FEET by 72 FEET	15 MINUTES
0.13 ACRES	75 FEET by 75 FEET	17 MINUTES
0.14 ACRES	78 FEET by 78 FEET	20 MINUTES
0.15 ACRES	81 FEET by 81 FEET	23 MINUTES
0.16 ACRES	84 FEET by 84 FEET	26 MINUTES
0.17 ACRES	86 FEET by 86 FEET	29 MINUTES
0.18 ACRES	89 FEET by 89 FEET	33 MINUTES
0.19 ACRES	91 FEET by 91 FEET	37 MINUTES
0.20 ACRES	93 FEET by 93 FEET	41 MINUTES
0.21 ACRES	96 FEET by 96 FEET	45 MINUTES
0.22 ACRES	98 FEET by 98 FEET	49 MINUTES
0.23 ACRES	100 FEET by 100 FEET	53 MINUTES
0.24 ACRES	102 FEET by 102 FEET	57 MINUTES
0.25 ACRES	104 FEET by 104 FEET	1 HOUR & 2 MINUTES
0.26 ACRES	106 FEET by 106 FEET	1 HOUR & 7 MINUTES
0.27 ACRES	108 FEET by 108 FEET	1 HOUR & 13 MINUTES
0.28 ACRES	110 FEET by 110 FEET	1 HOUR & 19 MINUTES
0.29 ACRES	112 FEET by 112 FEET	1 HOUR & 25 MINUTES
0.30 ACRES	114 FEET by 114 FEET	1 HOUR & 31 MINUTES
0.31 ACRES	116 FEET by 116 FEET	1 HOUR & 37 MINUTES
0.32 ACRES	118 FEET by 118 FEET	1 HOUR & 43 MINUTES
0.33 ACRES	120 FEET by 120 FEET	1 HOUR & 50 MINUTES
0.34 ACRES	122 FEET by 122 FEET	1 HOUR & 59 MINUTES
0.35 ACRES	124 FEET by 124 FEET	2 HOUR & 8 MINUTES
0.36 ACRES	125 FEET by 125 FEET	2 HOUR & 17 MINUTES
0.37 ACRES	127 FEET by 127 FEET	2 HOUR & 25 MINUTES

The mowing times given in the table are for a 20-inch mower. A more narrow, 18-inch mower would require about 10% additional mowing time. And a wider, 22-inch mower would require about 10% less mowing time.

Any one of these methods may be selected. Therefore, each one will be explained in detail.

ASKING "THE CUSTOMER" METHOD

How can you determine lot size or mowing time? It's simple. Ask the customer. Ask "What is the size of your house lot?" The customer can sometimes tell you the acreage. If not, then ask another question, "How long does it take to mow your lawn?" The customer can often tell you how long it takes, either from personal experience or from knowing how long it has taken another person to mow the lawn. Step one is usually this easy.

If the customer can't answer either one of the two questions, then, as an option, you could choose the equivalent-square method to estimate the size of the lot.

EQUIVALENT-SQUARE METHOD

To use the equivalent-square method, you must pace a house lot to determine its length and width dimensions. This takes only a few minutes. After doing this, the dimensions need to be converted to an equivalent-sized square lot (a square lot that would be equivalent in area to the rectangular lot). This also takes only a few minutes. Then, by looking in the MOWING TIME ESTIMATING TABLE, you can find the particular lot size (in acres) that corresponds with the equivalent-square dimensions. Here is the procedure:

Walk the length of the property counting your paces, and walk the width of the property counting your paces. Then multiply the number of paces by the distance of your pace. If your paces are two feet long, you would multiply the number of paces by two to determine the length and width in feet. Or, if you were to take long strides, say four feet long, then multiply by four instead of two. Basically, you need to know the distance of your pace and use that distance as a multiplier.

Should any property have a non-rectangular shape, apply your best judgment to get the average length and average width dimensions. After getting the dimensions, the MOWING TIME ESTIMATING TABLE is used to find the acreage of the lot. However, you will notice that the table gives dimensions for square lots only. Therefore, before using the table, the dimensions must be converted to an equivalent-sized square lot.

Here's how to make the conversion. Assume that you had just paced a lot which measured 90 feet by 110 feet. These dimensions are easily converted to an equivalent-sized square lot by taking the average distance between 90 and 110, which is 100 feet, and, as shown in the table, a property of 100 feet by 100 feet corresponds to a 0.23 acre lot (requiring 53 minutes of mowing time).

In this particular example, the two dimensions (of 90 and 110) were modified, or changed, by an average of about 10% to convert to a square lot (of 100 feet). Yet, the equivalent-sized square lot is very close to the same size as the rectangular lot. Consequently, when rectangular dimensions need to be modified by 10%, the equivalent-sized square lot is only one percent larger than the actual rectangular lot. Any modifications of less than 10% would be even more accurate, nearly perfect.

If the dimensions of a lot were to be 80 feet by 120 feet, again the equivalent-sized square lot would be 100 feet by 100 feet. (It's 100 again because 100 is the average, or half-way, distance between 80 and 120) But this conversion requires an average of about 21% modification of the two dimensions. As a result, the equivalent-sized square lot would be four percent larger than the actual rectangular lot. So an equivalent-sized square lot is still quite accurate, even with 21% modification of the dimensions.

Suppose the dimensions of a lot were to be 70 feet by 130 feet, where again, the equivalent-sized square lot would be 100 feet by 100 feet. In this case, the conversion would require an average of about 33% modification of the two dimensions. With this much modification the equivalent-sized square lot would be 10% larger than the actual rectangular lot. A 33% modification is approaching the limit for using the equivalent-square method. But allowing up to a 33% modification of rectangular dimensions will cover the great majority of house lots.

An easy way to know when not to use the equivalent-square method is: don't use it if the length of a house lot is more than twice the width. When the length is exactly twice the width, an equivalent-square lot is 12.5% larger than the actual rectangular lot. You shouldn't go beyond this point.

The accuracy of the equivalent-square method is shown in Figure 19.

An equivalent-sized square lot can also be determined by using a different approach. This approach is easier, and can be accomplished quicker. It saves you from having to modify from rectangular dimensions to square dimensions. It's called the equivalent-square, short-cut method.

EQUIVALENT-SQUARE, SHORT-CUT METHOD

This short-cut will work if, and only if, you adjust your steps to be about two feet long when pacing the dimensions of a house lot. This is the short-cut: Walk the length and width of a lot with approximately two-feet-long steps, counting the paces as you go along. Add both the number of length-paces and width-paces together. The total paces (of length and width added together) are also, by coincidence, the distance in feet of the sides of an equivalent-sized square lot. No conversion is necessary. You can go directly to the **MOWING TIME ESTIMATING TABLE** and find the corresponding lot-size (and associated mowing time).

An example of the short-cut will convince you that it works. Assume that a house lot is 80 feet wide by 120 feet long (where, from a previous example, the equivalent-sized square lot is already known to be 100 feet by 100 feet). By walking in two-foot length steps, the 80 feet width will be 40 paces and the 120 feet length will be 60 paces. The total paces (40 plus 60) equal 100, and therefore, the sides of the equivalent-sized square lot are 100 feet by 100 feet. It's a very simple short-cut.

WHEN USING THE EQUIVALENT-SQUARE METHOD

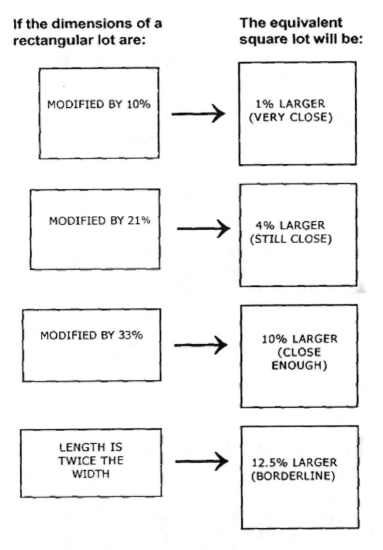

If the dimensions of a rectangular lot are:

The equivalent square lot will be:

| MODIFIED BY 10% | → | 1% LARGER (VERY CLOSE) |

| MODIFIED BY 21% | → | 4% LARGER (STILL CLOSE) |

| MODIFIED BY 33% | → | 10% LARGER (CLOSE ENOUGH) |

| LENGTH IS TWICE THE WIDTH | → | 12.5% LARGER (BORDERLINE) |

Don't use the Equivalent-Square method if the length of a lot is more than twice the width.

FIGURE 19. Accuracy of the Equivalent-Square Method

ACREAGE-MATRIX METHOD

This method requires that you pace a house lot to get its length and width dimensions. And then, use those dimensions to look up the acreage in the ACREAGE MATRIX (Figure 20). This matrix was devised as a result of calculating the acreage values for different-sized house lots of various dimensions. Hence the ACREAGE MATRIX is a tool for looking up the acreage of a house lot, once you know the length and width dimensions.

Observe the arrangement of the matrix: It will cover any house lot ranging from 50 to 180 feet in width and from 100 to 350 feet in length. To determine the acreage of a lot, after you have paced the length and width dimensions, look for the location in the table where the two dimensions intersect with each other. The acreage value is given at the intersection point.

Here are some examples: Let's assume that you had just paced a house lot that measured 80 feet wide by 150 feet long. The value of the acreage is given, where the column for 80 feet of width (going down) intersects with the row for 150 feet of length (going across). The size of this lot is 0.28 acres, as can been seen in the matrix. If a lot were to be 120 feet wide by 140 feet long, the location of intersection of these two dimensions shows that the size of this lot would be 0.39 acres. And, if a lot were 50 feet wide by 200 feet long, it would be a 0.23 acre lot. As can be seen, the matrix is quite easy to use.

ACREAGE-EQUATION METHOD

This method is purely mathematical and can be used if you have a pocket calculator. After having paced a house lot to determine its length and width dimensions, multiply the length times the width to calculate the number of square feet in the lot. Then divide by 43,560, which is the number of square feet in an acre. This will determine the acreage. The formula is given on page 68.

ACREAGE MATRIX

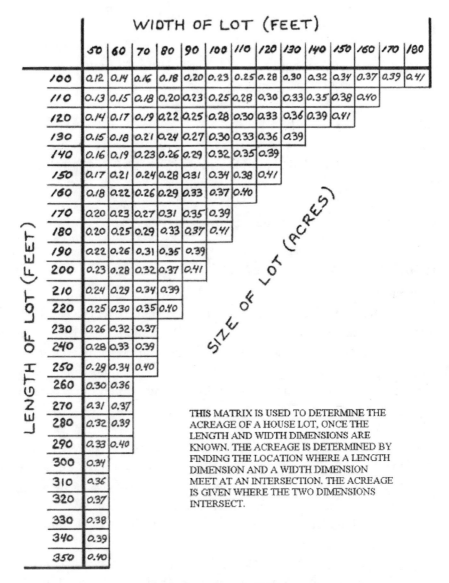

THIS MATRIX IS USED TO DETERMINE THE ACREAGE OF A HOUSE LOT, ONCE THE LENGTH AND WIDTH DIMENSIONS ARE KNOWN. THE ACREAGE IS DETERMINED BY FINDING THE LOCATION WHERE A LENGTH DIMENSION AND A WIDTH DIMENSION MEET AT AN INTERSECTION. THE ACREAGE IS GIVEN WHERE THE TWO DIMENSIONS INTERSECT.

FIGURE 20. Acreage Matrix

ACREAGE - EQUATION FORMULA

Acreage = <u>Width (in feet) times Length (in feet)</u>
divided by 43,560 (square feet per acre)

Example: By pacing, a lot is found to be 80 feet wide by 180 feet long.

Acreage = <u>(80 feet)(180 feet)</u>
43,560 square feet per acre

Acreage = 0.33 acres

By looking in the MOWING TIME ESTIMATING TABLE (Table 1), it can be seen that the mowing time which corresponds to 0.33 acres is one hour and 50 minutes. Therefore, you can quote a price based on either the size of the lot or the mowing time.

BRIEF REVIEW OF STEP ONE

Step one deserves a brief review: The only reason for estimating the size of lot (or the mowing time) is to assess how much work will be required. This can be done by using any one of the methods that have been described. However, the most obvious method is to start by asking the customer. Most often this is all that's required. And then you're ready to quote a price. But, if the customer doesn't know either the lot size or the mowing time, you can estimate it yourself.

No matter which method is used, the first thing you have to do is pace the house lot. Get its length and width dimensions. Once the dimensions are known, you can determine the size of the lot by using either the equivalent-square method, the acreage-matrix method, or the acreage-equation method. They all work. Use whichever method makes you feel most comfortable.

It's not necessary to hurry when estimating. In fact, you can take your time about it. Customers realize that a job can't be estimated immediately. And they don't mind waiting while you do it. Nevertheless, any method used will require only about five minutes, or less, to estimate the size of a house lot.

After having mowed many properties, you'll be able to readily estimate the lot-size or mowing time quite closely, just by observations. This comes with experience.

ESTIMATING, STEP TWO

Step two requires having a price list. You need to have a set of prices for different sizes of lots and mowing times. Therefore, this step is very simple, after you have established the prices that you're going to charge. Since prices are sensitive, be aware that it's possible to charge a small enough fee to get all the customers you want, and more besides. But, with low profit margins, there would be no incentive to work, particularly if you put yourself in a position where you're working for practically nothing. And it is also possible to charge such high prices that you wouldn't get any customers at all. Your services would be too expensive.

So then, how much should you charge? Charge the most profitable prices that the majority of customers are willing to pay. How can you know what these prices are? There are two ways to get the information. Find out for yourself the hard way, by trial and error, and be prepared because it can be a time-consuming task. Or, do it the easy way. Consider using price data that has been evaluated from experience and predetermined for you.

This is where it now becomes worthwhile to review some already-established prices.

The prices which will be given could be, but are not necessarily, applicable to your particular neighborhood. The prices in your area may be somewhat higher or lower, depending on demand and other local variables. Therefore, consider the prices that will be quoted from experience in Massachusetts as being guidelines. But also, since the location from where the price data was taken had levels of employment and levels of income which ran close to the national average, the rates, in general, may very well apply in most other areas.

Prices will be given in 1981 dollars, but there's no need for concern as to what the equivalent, present-day prices would be. At the end of this chapter there are several different price estimating tables to guide you, each year, to keep up with inflation. An explanation of these tables will be covered after first reviewing the 1981 (baseline year) price data. This data was established from actual payments which were received from the customers shown in the examples.

PAYMENTS RECEIVED

The payments (or prices) which were received from the customers are shown in the PAYMENTS bar chart (Figure 21). Notice how the payments keep increasing as the sizes of the house lots increase, over the range from 0.12 acres (15 minutes of mowing time) to 0.24 acres (one hour of mowing time). And then see how the payments level off.

From 0.24 acres (one hour of mowing time) up to 0.34 acres (two hours of mowing time), the payments remain relatively constant, at $10. Or, in other words, customers are willing to pay about the same price for house lots that range between one hour and two hours of mowing time. This is an interesting trend to be aware of. You can make the same amount of money in one hour as you can in two hours. This trend alerts you to put an emphasis on trying to get more of the one-hour jobs than the two-hour jobs, as a means of maximizing profits.

The payment didn't jump above the $10 level until the size of a house lot reached 0.37 acres (nearly two and one-half hours of mowing time). At this point, the pay was $15.

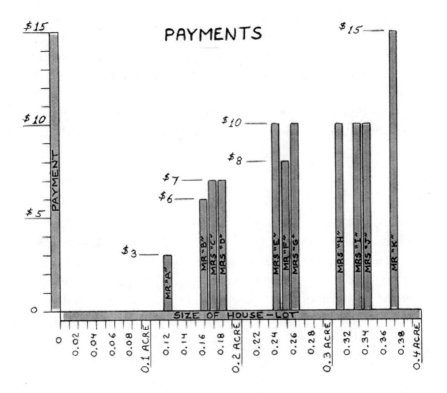

The bar chart shows payments that were received for mowing various sizes of house lots. Each bar's vertical height represents the payment received. As can be seen, the pay increases as the size of the house lot increases, but only to a point, and then levels off. For house lots ranging from 0.12 acres up to 0.24 acres, the pay keeps increasing. This can be seen by looking at the payments received from Mr. "A", Mr. "B", Mrs. "C", Mrs. "D", and Mrs. "E".

However, for five of the six house lots between 0.24 acres and 0.34 acres, the pay leveled off to $10.00. This can be seen by looking at the payments received from Mrs. "F", Mrs. "G", Mrs. "H", Mrs. "I", and Mrs. "J". The pay did not jump to $15 until the lot size reached 0.37 acres. This is the house lot of Mr. "K".

The payments are in 1981 dollars.

FIGURE 21. Payments Bar Chart

Therefore, the analytical profile of the data shows that prices increase rather dramatically for small lots, up to about one hour of mowing. After that, prices level off for lots requiring between one hour and two hours of mowing time. And, prices do not increase any further until lot sizes approach somewhere between two hours and two and one-half hours of mowing time.

Also of interest is to know how much earning power can be associated with various sizes of house lots. Earning power can be evaluated by determining the hourly rates of pay for each lot size.

HOURLY RATES OF PAY

By using a simple cost analysis technique, it is easy to evaluate how much money can be earned on an hourly basis. The hourly rates of pay have been calculated as a result of dividing the payment by the mowing time. This was done for each house lot. For example, consider the property of Mr. "A". It took 15 minutes (or, one-fourth of an hour) to mow his lawn. The payment was $3. So, the hourly rate of pay for his lot was $3 divided by one-fourth of an hour, which is $12 per hour.

Since the size of Mr. "A's" property is 0.12 acres, the hourly rate of pay for this lot size is $12 an hour. In conclusion, the earning power, or hourly rate of pay, for a 0.12 acre lot is $12 per hour. This same type of calculation was made for each of the properties that were given in the examples. The results of the analysis can be seen in the HOURLY RATES OF PAY bar chart (Figure 22). The chart exposes the sizes of house lots which are most profitable, showing where you can make the greatest amount of money in the least amount of time. It shows quite clearly that the smallest lots are the most profitable.

Lots between 0.12 acres (15 minutes of mowing time) and 0.18 acres (35 minutes of mowing time) provide the highest pay rates; these are the most profitable lots. They paid from $12 to $14 an hour.

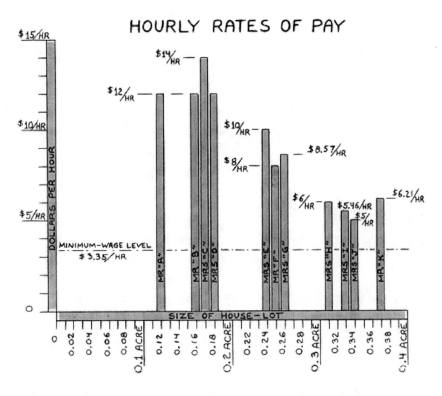

The bar chart shows the hourly rates of pay for various sizes of house lots. Each bar's vertical height represents the amount of dollars per hour

Notice how the hourly rates of pay decrease as the size of the house lots increase. Clearly the smaller lots of less than one-quarter acre offer the highest profits. And these properties require only an hour or less of mowing time.

However, the hourly rates of pay for the larger lots are still attractive when compared with the minimum wage of $3.35 per hour. The four largest lots have an average pay rate which is close to twice the minimum wage.

The hourly rates of pay and minimum-wage are in 1981 dollars.

FIGURE 22. Hourly Rates of Pay Bar Chart

For all larger sizes of house lots, the hourly rates of pay keep decreasing as the lots get larger. However, all lots of less than 0.25 acres pay quite well. And these properties require only an hour or less of mowing time. About half of all your customers will probably be in this category.

It's also worth noting that the hourly rates of pay for the larger sized lots are not insignificant. They paid considerably more than the $3.35 federal minimum wage level. All customers paid much more than the minimum wage level. This holds true, at least, until the sizes of house lots get to be about 0.4 acres. This is the cutoff point.

LOTS LARGER THAN 0.4 ACRES

There is a practical limit on the sizes of house lots that you should mow. When lot sizes reach 0.4 acres, they require about three hours of mowing time. At this point many customers tend to think in terms of paying by the hour rather than by the job. And they think in terms of low rates, close to the minimum wage level.

For example, not included in the data was a motel with a half-acre lot where the owner offered to pay only slightly more than the minimum wage. There was also a lodging house with a. two-acre lot where the owner offered to pay just slightly less than the minimum wage. Another owner, of a private school with a three-acre lot, also offered to pay less than the minimum wage.

The only way that large lots can become profitable is by making a big investment. You would need to purchase a wide-cutting lawn tractor. One of these mowers could easily be two to four times faster than walking behind a rotary push mower. With a fast-cutting rig like this, yes, customers who have lot sizes of 0.4 acres and larger will definitely pay by the job as opposed to paying by the hour. A large 16-horsepower model will handle just about any mowing job with ease. But, as you can imagine, a wide-cutting lawn tractor is expensive.

Unfortunately, to pay for a big investment takes time. And trying to make quick financial recovery of your investment may necessitate going into the mowing business on a more demanding scale. This could mean having to go after some of the large commercial jobs which sometimes require formal bidding procedures, negotiation of firm commitments, and the signing of contracts. It can be an arena of stiff competition.

This aspect of the mowing business is beyond the scope and intent of this book. That's why the data has been limited to lot sizes of less than 0.4 acres.

You're better off with smaller-sized lots. They're a wide open market with very little or no competition. There is plenty of incentive for making good money. And only a modest investment is required, that is, if you don't already own a lawn mower.

Once you've gained experience in dealing with customers and have become an expert in pricing the jobs, then you'll be in a better position if you want to consider investing in a large mower. By this time, assuming that you're ambitious, it's quite likely you will have earned a bundle of money. You'll be amazed at how fast you can accumulate income.

For example, an average rate of pay for the 11 customers which were shown in the examples was $9.02 an hour. This is 2.7 times the 1981 minimum wage rate. Therefore, the average rate of pay that the majority of customers are willing to pay for lawn mowing services is about 270% of the minimum wage level.

There is a very important reason for knowing the percentages of pay rates (for various lot sizes) with respect to the minimum wage. These relationships can be used to project future prices beyond 1981. Projecting future prices will require that the pay rates always be kept at the same percentage levels above the minimum wage; each time the minimum wage is increased, consequently, price estimating tables can be prepared on this basis.

PRICE ESTIMATING TABLES, GENERAL DESCRIPTION

Historically, the Federal government has increased the minimum wage guidelines on an average of about every 3.5 years (see Figure 23). This is done in an attempt to keep pace with inflation. Whenever this happens, the prices for mowing lawns can be increased proportionately in order to remain at a constant percentage level above the minimum wage. Even though this may seem simple enough to do, it's much easier said than done.

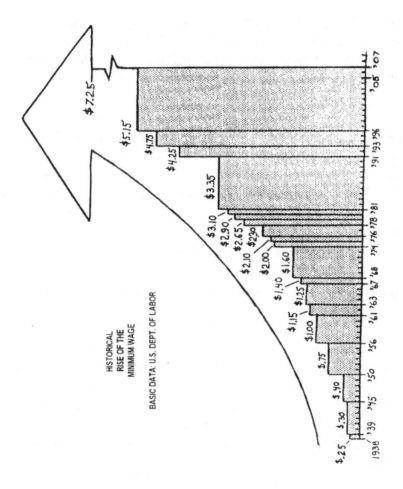

FIGURE 23. Historical Rise of the Minimum Wage

For this reason many different PRICE ESTIMATING TABLES have been prepared for you. They're in Tables 2 through 22 at the end of this chapter.

Each table stands alone to give an independent set of prices which will apply for a particular forthcoming minimum wage rate. During any given mowing season, you would need to be concerned with only one of the tables -- whichever one applies to the current minimum wage. If you don't know the current minimum wage, call a local business firm, newspaper office, or your local unemployment agency. They can tell you. Or, you could go to the U.S. Dept. of Labor web-site, which gives the current Federal Minimum Wage; and, also minimum wages for some states that provide their own minimum wage guidelines. The web-site address is:

http://www.dol.gov/esa/minwage/america.htm

If your state has its own separate minimum wage guideline, then you should default to your own specific state. It should take preference.

There are 21 PRICE ESTIMATING TABLES. The first table (Table 2) shows the prices which were established in 1981, at the time when the minimum wage was $3.35 an hour. The second table (Table 3) shows an escalated set of prices for the minimum wage of $5.15 an hour. The third table (Table 4) shows an escalated set of prices for when the minimum wage will have reached exactly (or about) $5.50 an hour. The fourth table (Table 5) and each table thereafter, continue to show higher escalated sets of prices for ever-increasing values of the minimum wage. The tables progress in 50¢ increments.

The data in these tables is structured so that you can quote prices either by the size of a house lot or the mowing time.

It should be emphasized that increases in prices are not based on any anticipated inflation rates from one year to the next. This would be impossible to predict with any reasonable degree of accuracy. That's why price increases were based on increasing values of the minimum wage. It's quite reasonable to assume that customers will continue to pay prices that reflect the same consistent percentage levels above the minimum wage. Or, if your state has its own minimum wage guideline, then always go by your own state. A state minimum wage should take preference over the Federal minimum wage as a guideline.

It is possible that the prices in the tables could become somewhat conservative if annual inflation rates were to rise much faster than government increases in the minimum wage. However, should this occur and you feel that the prices in the tables become too low, try raising your prices. If you are able to get higher prices, this certainly is no problem. Under these special conditions, consider the tables as giving the minimum prices you should charge.

PRICE ESTIMATING TABLES, DETAILED DESCRIPTION

The PRICE ESTIMATING TABLES were devised as a result of having combined selected elements of data from the MOWING TIME ESTI-MATING TABLE, the PAYMENTS bar chart, the HOURLY RATES OF PAY bar chart, and also, as a result of having made escalation adjust-ments of prices to keep pace with increasing values of the minimum wage. To simplify the tables as much as possible, they were made to show only six major categories of house lots. The categories were divided so as to include lot sizes which require 1/4 hour, 1/2 hour, 1 hour, 1 1/2 hours, 2 hours, and 2 1/2 hours of mowing time. These mowing times cover the range of small house lots from 0.12 acres to 0.37 acres.

All the PRICE ESTIMATING TABLES are of identical format and contain the same column titles of information. Going from left to right, the first column gives the "size of a house lot" in terms of the "area" (in "acres"). The second column also gives the size of a house lot, but in terms of the "dimensions" (in "feet") and the third column gives the mowing time (in "hours"). These first three columns represent standard information which is repeated in every table. The fourth column gives the "prices". The prices are different in every table. This is because each table contains a unique set of prices that will apply to a particular minimum wage value. Therefore, simply select the PRICE ESTIMATING TABLE that applies to the current value of the minimum wage.

The first table (TABLE 2) is not used; it is there only to preserve the original price data. TABLES 3 through 22 show an escalated set of prices for various, increased values of the minimum wage.

Note that the prices in the PRICE ESTIMATING TABLES were calculated to the nearest penny. If you find it more convenient to round off prices to the nearest quarter, half dollar, or dollar value, then do it. This is left to your own discretion.

The first four columns in each table, which give the house lot size, the mowing time, and the prices, will provide all the information for determining prices.

The fifth and sixth columns have been included in the tables only for the purpose of providing special additional information. They're not used for determining prices. That's why they have been shown with dotted lines. What these columns do is provide you with some insight into the degree of profitability.

The fifth column gives the "Hourly Rate of Pay" that is associated with the various sizes of house lots. These rates of pay allow you to see the sizes of lots which are most profitable, showing where you can earn the most money in the least amount of time. Observe that the pay rates decrease as the size of house lots increase, and therefore, that the smallest lots are the most profitable.

The sixth column gives the "Hourly Rate Compared to the Minimum Wage". This column shows how much more profitable it is, on an hourly basis, to be mowing lawns than it would be if you were working for someone else at the minimum wage. The comparison is made for each of the different sizes of house lots. Note that the comparison is expressed as a percentage; that is, if a rate of pay were to be two times the minimum wage rate, then this comparison would be 200% of the minimum wage.

In making these comparisons, the hourly rates of pay (given in the fifth column) were divided by the minimum wage value. For example, in the first PRICE ESTIMATING TABLE (Table 2), which is for a minimum wage of $3.35 per hour, the comparison for a 0.12 acre lot was made as follows: The hourly rate of pay (of $12/hr.) was divided by the minimum wage (of $3.35/hr.). This gives a comparison ratio of 3.58, which when converted to a percentage value is 358%. Thus, in the sixth column, for a 0.12 acre lot, it shows that the hourly rate of pay for mowing lawns is 358% of the minimum wage rate of pay. This gives you some perspective on profitability.

Now, as a quick summary of this chapter, estimating takes place in two basic steps. Step one involves determining either the size of a lot or the mowing time. Step two is to have a set of prices which represent the most profitable fees that the majority of customers are willing to pay. The PRICE ESTIMATING TABLES (which begin on the following page) give you this information. Use the table which applies nearest to the current minimum wage.

This table is retained so as to preserve the original baseline price data

SIZE OF HOUSE LOT		MOWING TIME	PRICE	HOURLY RATE OF PAY	HOURLY RATE COMPARED TO MINIMUM WAGE
AREA	DIMENSIONS (IF LOT WERE SQUARE)				
0.12 acres	72 ft. by 72 ft.	¼ hour	$3.00	$12/hr.	358%
0.17 acres	86 ft. by 86 ft.	½ hour	$6.00	$12/hr.	358%
0.25 acres	104 ft. by 104 ft.	1 hour	$10.00	$10/hr.	299%
0.30 acres	114 ft. by 114 ft.	1½ hours	$10.00	$6.67/hr.	199%
0.34 acres	122 ft. by 122 ft.	2 hours	$10.00	$5/hr.	149%
0.37 acres	127 ft. by 127 ft.	2½ hours	$15.00	$6/hr.	179%

TABLE 2.
PRICE ESTIMATING TABLE
For a minimum wage of $3.35 per hour

Size of House Lot		Mowing Time	Price	Hourly Rate of Pay	Hourly Rate Compared to Minimum Wage
Area	Dimensions (if lot were square)				
0.12 acres	72 ft. by 72 ft.	$\frac{1}{4}$ hour	$4.60	$18.40/hr.	358%
0.17 acres	86 ft. by 86 ft.	$\frac{1}{2}$ hour	$9.22	$18.40/hr.	358%
0.25 acres	104 ft. by 104 ft.	1 hour	$15.37	$15.37/hr.	299%
0.30 acres	114 ft. by 114 ft.	$1\frac{1}{2}$ hours	$15.37	$10.25/hr.	199%
0.34 acres	122 ft. by 122 ft.	2 hours	$15.37	$7.68/hr.	149%
0.37 acres	127 ft. by 127 ft.	$2\frac{1}{2}$ hours	$23.05	$9.22/hr.	179%

TABLE 3.
PRICE ESTIMATING TABLE
For a minimum wage of $5.15 per hour

Size of House Lot		Mowing Time	Price	Hourly Rate of Pay	Hourly Rate Compared to Minimum Wage
Area	Dimensions (if lot were square)				
0.12 acres	72 ft. by 72 ft.	$\frac{1}{4}$ hour	$4.93	$19.70/hr.	358%
0.17 acres	86 ft. by 86 ft.	$\frac{1}{2}$ hour	$9.85	$19.70/hr.	358%
0.25 acres	104 ft. by 104 ft.	1 hour	$16.42	$16.42/hr.	299%
0.30 acres	114 ft. by 114 ft.	$1\frac{1}{2}$ hours	$16.42	$10.95/hr.	199%
0.34 acres	122 ft. by 122 ft.	2 hours	$16.42	$8.21/hr.	149%
0.37 acres	127 ft. by 127 ft.	$2\frac{1}{2}$ hours	$24.63	$9.85/hr.	179%

TABLE 4.
PRICE ESTIMATING TABLE
For a minimum wage of $5.50 per hour

Size of House Lot		Mowing Time	Price	Hourly Rate of Pay	Hourly Rate Compared to Minimum Wage
Area	Dimensions (if lot were square)				
0.12 acres	72 ft. by 72 ft.	¼ hour	$5.37	$21.49/hr.	358%
0.17 acres	86 ft. by 86 ft.	½ hour	$10.75	$21.49/hr.	358%
0.25 acres	104 ft. by 104 ft.	1 hour	$17.92	$17.92/hr.	299%
0.30 acres	114 ft. by 114 ft.	1½ hours	$17.92	$11.95/hr.	199%
0.34 acres	122 ft. by 122 ft.	2 hours	$17.92	$8.96/hr.	149%
0.37 acres	127 ft. by 127 ft.	2½ hours	$26.87	$10.75/hr.	179%

TABLE 5.

PRICE ESTIMATING TABLE

For a minimum wage of $6.00 per hour

Size of House Lot		Mowing Time	Price	Hourly Rate of Pay	Hourly Rate Compared to Minimum Wage
Area	Dimensions (if lot were square)				
0.12 acres	72 ft. by 72 ft.	¼ hour	$5.82	$23.28/hr.	358%
0.17 acres	86 ft. by 86 ft.	½ hour	$11.64	$23.28/hr.	358%
0.25 acres	104 ft. by 104 ft.	1 hour	$19.41	$19.41/hr.	299%
0.30 acres	114 ft. by 114 ft.	1½ hours	$19.41	$12.94/hr.	199%
0.34 acres	122 ft. by 122 ft.	2 hours	$19.41	$9.70/hr.	149%
0.37 acres	127 ft. by 127 ft.	2½ hours	$29.10	$11.64/hr.	179%

TABLE 6.

PRICE ESTIMATING

For a minimum wage of $6.50 per hour

Size of House Lot		Mowing Time	Price	Hourly Rate of Pay	Hourly Rate Compared to Minimum Wage
Area	Dimensions (if lot were square)				
0.12 acres	72 ft. by 72 ft.	$\frac{1}{4}$ hour	$6.27	$25.07/hr.	358%
0.17 acres	86 ft. by 86 ft.	$\frac{1}{2}$ hour	$12.54	$25.07/hr.	358%
0.25 acres	104 ft. by 104 ft.	1 hour	$20.90	$20.90/hr.	299%
0.30 acres	114 ft. by 114 ft.	$1\frac{1}{2}$ hours	$20.90	$13.94/hr.	199%
0.34 acres	122 ft. by 122 ft.	2 hours	$20.90	$10.45/hr.	149%
0.37 acres	127 ft. by 127 ft.	$2\frac{1}{2}$ hours	$31.34	$12.54/hr.	179%

TABLE 7.

PRICE ESTIMATING TABLE

For a minimum wage of $7.00 per hour

Size of House Lot		Mowing Time	Price	Hourly Rate of Pay	Hourly Rate Compared to Minimum Wage
Area	Dimensions (if lot were square)				
0.12 acres	72 ft. by 72 ft.	$\frac{1}{4}$ hour	$6.72	$26.87/hr.	358%
0.17 acres	86 ft. by 86 ft.	$\frac{1}{2}$ hour	$13.43	$26.87/hr.	358%
0.25 acres	104 ft. by 104 ft.	1 hour	$22.40	$22.40/hr.	299%
0.30 acres	114 ft. by 114 ft.	$1\frac{1}{2}$ hours	$22.40	$14.93/hr.	199%
0.34 acres	122 ft. by 122 ft.	2 hours	$22.40	$11.20/hr.	149%
0.37 acres	127 ft. by 127 ft.	$2\frac{1}{2}$ hours	$33.58	$13.43/hr.	179%

TABLE 8.

PRICE ESTIMATING TABLE

For a minimum wage of $7.50 per hour

SIZE OF HOUSE LOT		MOWING TIME	PRICE	HOURLY RATE OF PAY	HOURLY RATE COMPARED TO MINIMUM WAGE
AREA	DIMENSIONS (IF LOT WERE SQUARE)				
0.12 acres	72 ft. by 72 ft.	$\frac{1}{4}$ hour	$7.16	$28.66/hr.	358%
0.17 acres	86 ft. by 86 ft.	$\frac{1}{2}$ hour	$14.33	$28.66/hr.	358%
0.25 acres	104 ft. by 104 ft.	1 hour	$23.89	$23.89/hr.	299%
0.30 acres	114 ft. by 114 ft.	1$\frac{1}{2}$ hours	$23.89	$15.93/hr.	199%
0.34 acres	122 ft. by 122 ft.	2 hours	$23.89	$11.94/hr.	149%
0.37 acres	127 ft. by 127 ft.	2$\frac{1}{2}$ hours	$35.82	$14.33/hr.	179%

TABLE 9.

PRICE ESTIMATING TABLE

For a minimum wage of $8.00 per hour

SIZE OF HOUSE LOT		MOWING TIME	PRICE	HOURLY RATE OF PAY	HOURLY RATE COMPARED TO MINIMUM WAGE
AREA	DIMENSIONS (IF LOT WERE SQUARE)				
0.12 acres	72 ft. by 72 ft.	$\frac{1}{4}$ hour	$7.61	$30.45/hr.	358%
0.17 acres	86 ft. by 86 ft.	$\frac{1}{2}$ hour	$15.22	$30.45/hr.	358%
0.25 acres	104 ft. by 104 ft.	1 hour	$25.37	$25.37/hr.	299%
0.30 acres	114 ft. by 114 ft.	1$\frac{1}{2}$ hours	$25.39	$16.92/hr.	199%
0.34 acres	122 ft. by 122 ft.	2 hours	$25.38	$12.69/hr.	149%
0.37 acres	127 ft. by 127 ft.	2$\frac{1}{2}$ hours	$38.06	$15.22/hr.	179%

TABLE 10.

PRICE ESTIMATING TABLE

For a minimum wage of $8.50 per hour

Size of House Lot		Mowing Time	Price	Hourly Rate of Pay	Hourly Rate Compared to Minimum Wage
Area	Dimensions (if lot were square)				
0.12 acres	72 ft. by 72 ft.	$\frac{1}{4}$ hour	$8.06	$32.24/hr.	358%
0.17 acres	86 ft. by 86 ft.	$\frac{1}{2}$ hour	$16.12	$32.24/hr.	358%
0.25 acres	104 ft. by 104 ft.	1 hour	$26.87	$26.87/hr.	299%
0.30 acres	114 ft. by 114 ft.	$1\frac{1}{2}$ hours	$26.88	$17.92/hr.	199%
0.34 acres	122 ft. by 122 ft.	2 hours	$26.87	$13.44/hr.	149%
0.37 acres	127 ft. by 127 ft.	$2\frac{1}{2}$ hours	$40.30	$16.12/hr.	179%

TABLE 11.
PRICE ESTIMATING TABLE
For a minimum wage of $9.00 per hour

Size of House Lot		Mowing Time	Price	Hourly Rate of Pay	Hourly Rate Compared to Minimum Wage
Area	Dimensions (if lot were square)				
0.12 acres	72 ft. by 72 ft.	$\frac{1}{4}$ hour	$8.50	$34.00/hr.	358%
0.17 acres	86 ft. by 86 ft.	$\frac{1}{2}$ hour	$17.40	$34.08/hr.	358%
0.25 acres	104 ft. by 104 ft.	1 hour	$28.40	$28.40/hr.	299%
0.30 acres	114 ft. by 114 ft.	$1\frac{1}{2}$ hours	$28.40	$18.93/hr.	199%
0.34 acres	122 ft. by 122 ft.	2 hours	$28.40	$14.20/hr.	149%
0.37 acres	127 ft. by 127 ft.	$2\frac{1}{2}$ hours	$42.60	$17.04/hr.	179%

TABLE 12.
PRICE ESTIMATING TABLE
For a minimum wage of $9.50 per hour

| SIZE OF HOUSE LOT | | MOWING TIME | PRICE | HOURLY RATE OF PAY | HOURLY RATE COMPARED TO MINIMUM WAGE |
AREA	DIMENSIONS (IF LOT WERE SQUARE)				
0.12 acres	72 ft. by 72 ft.	$\frac{1}{4}$ hour	$8.97	$35.88/hr.	358%
0.17 acres	86 ft. by 86 ft.	$\frac{1}{2}$ hour	$17.94	$35.88/hr.	358%
0.25 acres	104 ft. by 104 ft.	1 hour	$29.90	$29.90/hr.	299%
0.30 acres	114 ft. by 114 ft.	1$\frac{1}{2}$ hours	$29.90	$19.93/hr.	199%
0.34 acres	122 ft. by 122 ft.	2 hours	$29.90	$14.95/hr.	149%
0.37 acres	127 ft. by 127 ft.	2$\frac{1}{2}$ hours	$44.85	$17.94/hr.	179%

TABLE 13.

PRICE ESTIMATING TABLE

For a minimum wage of $10.00 per hour

| SIZE OF HOUSE LOT | | MOWING TIME | PRICE | HOURLY RATE OF PAY | HOURLY RATE COMPARED TO MINIMUM WAGE |
AREA	DIMENSIONS (IF LOT WERE SQUARE)				
0.12 acres	72 ft. by 72 ft.	$\frac{1}{4}$ hour	$9.40	$37.60/hr.	358%
0.17 acres	86 ft. by 86 ft.	$\frac{1}{2}$ hour	$18.80	$37.60/hr.	358%
0.25 acres	104 ft. by 104 ft.	1 hour	$31.34	$31.34/hr.	299%
0.30 acres	114 ft. by 114 ft.	1$\frac{1}{2}$ hours	$31.34	$20.89/hr.	199%
0.34 acres	122 ft. by 122 ft.	2 hours	$31.34	$15.67/hr.	149%
0.37 acres	127 ft. by 127 ft.	2$\frac{1}{2}$ hours	$47.01	$18.80/hr.	179%

TABLE 14.

PRICE ESTIMATING TABLE

For a minimum wage of $10.50 per hour

Size of House Lot		Mowing Time	Price	Hourly Rate of Pay	Hourly Rate Compared to Minimum Wage
Area	Dimensions (if lot were square)				
0.12 acres	72 ft. by 72 ft.	$\frac{1}{4}$ hour	$9.84	$39.36/hr.	358%
0.17 acres	86 ft. by 86 ft.	$\frac{1}{2}$ hour	$19.70	$39.36/hr.	358%
0.25 acres	104 ft. by 104 ft.	1 hour	$32.84	$32.84/hr.	299%
0.30 acres	114 ft. by 114 ft.	$1\frac{1}{2}$ hours	$32.84	$21.89/hr.	199%
0.34 acres	122 ft. by 122 ft.	2 hours	$32.84	$16.42/hr.	149%
0.37 acres	127 ft. by 127 ft.	$2\frac{1}{2}$ hours	$49.26	$19.70/hr.	179%

TABLE 15.
PRICE ESTIMATING TABLE
For a minimum wage of $11.00 per hour

Size of House Lot		Mowing Time	Price	Hourly Rate of Pay	Hourly Rate Compared to Minimum Wage
Area	Dimensions (if lot were square)				
0.12 acres	72 ft. by 72 ft.	$\frac{1}{4}$ hour	$10.33	$41.34/hr.	358%
0.17 acres	86 ft. by 86 ft.	$\frac{1}{2}$ hour	$20.66	$41.34/hr.	358%
0.25 acres	104 ft. by 104 ft.	1 hour	$34.33	$34.33/hr.	299%
0.30 acres	114 ft. by 114 ft.	$1\frac{1}{2}$ hours	$34.33	$22.88/hr.	199%
0.34 acres	122 ft. by 122 ft.	2 hours	$34.33	$17.17/hr.	149%
0.37 acres	127 ft. by 127 ft.	$2\frac{1}{2}$ hours	$51.49	$20.60/hr.	179%

TABLE 16.
PRICE ESTIMATING TABLE
For a minimum wage of $11.50 per hour

Size of House Lot		Mowing Time	Price	Hourly Rate of Pay	Hourly Rate Compared to Minimum Wage
Area	Dimensions (if lot were square)				
0.12 acres	72 ft. by 72 ft.	$\frac{1}{4}$ hour	$10.75	$43.00/hr.	358%
0.17 acres	86 ft. by 86 ft.	$\frac{1}{2}$ hour	$21.50	$43.00/hr.	358%
0.25 acres	104 ft. by 104 ft.	1 hour	$35.82	$35.82/hr.	299%
0.30 acres	114 ft. by 114 ft.	1$\frac{1}{2}$ hours	$35.82	$23.88/hr.	199%
0.34 acres	122 ft. by 122 ft.	2 hours	$35.82	$17.91/hr.	149%
0.37 acres	127 ft. by 127 ft.	2$\frac{1}{2}$ hours	$53.73	$21.49/hr.	179%

TABLE 17.

PRICE ESTIMATING TABLE

For a minimum wage of $12.00 per hour

Size of House Lot		Mowing Time	Price	Hourly Rate of Pay	Hourly Rate Compared to Minimum Wage
Area	Dimensions (if lot were square)				
0.12 acres	72 ft. by 72 ft.	$\frac{1}{4}$ hour	$11.19	$44.76/hr.	358%
0.17 acres	86 ft. by 86 ft.	$\frac{1}{2}$ hour	$22.38	$44.76/hr.	358%
0.25 acres	104 ft. by 104 ft.	1 hour	$37.30	$37.30/hr.	299%
0.30 acres	114 ft. by 114 ft.	1$\frac{1}{2}$ hours	$37.30	$24.87/hr.	199%
0.34 acres	122 ft. by 122 ft.	2 hours	$37.30	$18.65/hr.	149%
0.37 acres	127 ft. by 127 ft.	2$\frac{1}{2}$ hours	$55.95	$22.38/hr.	179%

TABLE 18.

PRICE ESTIMATING TABLE

For a minimum wage of $12.50 per hour

Size of House Lot		Mowing Time	Price	Hourly Rate of Pay	Hourly Rate Compared to Minimum Wage
Area	Dimensions (if lot were square)				
0.12 acres	72 ft. by 72 ft.	¼ hour	$11.64	$46.56/hr.	358%
0.17 acres	86 ft. by 86 ft.	½ hour	$23.28	$46.56/hr.	358%
0.25 acres	104 ft. by 104 ft.	1 hour	$38.80	$38.80/hr.	299%
0.30 acres	114 ft. by 114 ft.	1½ hours	$38.80	$25.87/hr.	199%
0.34 acres	122 ft. by 122 ft.	2 hours	$38.80	$19.40/hr.	149%
0.37 acres	127 ft. by 127 ft.	2½ hours	$58.20	$23.28/hr.	179%

TABLE 19.

PRICE ESTIMATING TABLE

For a minimum wage of $13.00 per hour

Size of House Lot		Mowing Time	Price	Hourly Rate of Pay	Hourly Rate Compared to Minimum Wage
Area	Dimensions (if lot were square)				
0.12 acres	72 ft. by 72 ft.	¼ hour	$12.05	$48.20/hr.	358%
0.17 acres	86 ft. by 86 ft.	½ hour	$24.10	$48.20/hr.	358%
0.25 acres	104 ft. by 104 ft.	1 hour	$40.30	$40.30/hr.	299%
0.30 acres	114 ft. by 114 ft.	1½ hours	$40.30	$26.87/hr.	199%
0.34 acres	122 ft. by 122 ft.	2 hours	$40.30	$20.15/hr.	149%
0.37 acres	127 ft. by 127 ft.	2½ hours	$60.45	$24.18/hr.	179%

TABLE 20.

PRICE ESTIMATING TABLE

For a minimum wage of $13.50 per hour

Size of House Lot		Mowing Time	Price	Hourly Rate of Pay	Hourly Rate Compared to Minimum Wage
Area	Dimensions (if lot were square)				
0.12 acres	72 ft. by 72 ft.	$\frac{1}{4}$ hour	$12.54	$50.16/hr.	358%
0.17 acres	86 ft. by 86 ft.	$\frac{1}{2}$ hour	$25.08	$50.16/hr.	358%
0.25 acres	104 ft. by 104 ft.	1 hour	$41.79	$41.79/hr.	299%
0.30 acres	114 ft. by 114 ft.	$1\frac{1}{2}$ hours	$41.79	$27.86/hr.	199%
0.34 acres	122 ft. by 122 ft.	2 hours	$41.79	$20.99/hr.	149%
0.37 acres	127 ft. by 127 ft.	$2\frac{1}{2}$ hours	$62.69	$25.08/hr.	179%

TABLE 21.
PRICE ESTIMATING TABLE
For a minimum wage of $14.00 per hour

Size of House Lot		Mowing Time	Price	Hourly Rate of Pay	Hourly Rate Compared to Minimum Wage
Area	Dimensions (if lot were square)				
0.12 acres	72 ft. by 72 ft.	$\frac{1}{4}$ hour	$12.98	$51.92/hr.	358%
0.17 acres	86 ft. by 86 ft.	$\frac{1}{2}$ hour	$25.96	$51.92/hr.	358%
0.25 acres	104 ft. by 104 ft.	1 hour	$43.28	$43.28/hr.	299%
0.30 acres	114 ft. by 114 ft.	$1\frac{1}{2}$ hours	$43.28	$28.85/hr.	199%
0.34 acres	122 ft. by 122 ft.	2 hours	$43.28	$21.64/hr.	149%
0.37 acres	127 ft. by 127 ft.	$2\frac{1}{2}$ hours	$64.92	$25.97/hr.	179%

TABLE 22.
PRICE ESTIMATING TABLE
For a minimum wage of $14.50 per hour

CHAPTER 5

SCHEDULING

One of the easiest ways to be well organized is to have a schedule. A schedule allows you to efficiently keep track of all your business activity on a single sheet of paper. Very little effort is involved. Detailed book work is not required. The more customers that you have, the more need there will be to have a schedule.

If you were to have only five or six customers, it wouldn't be necessary to have a schedule. Just about anyone can keep track of this many customers in his/her head. But, if you should have seven, eight or nine customers, it becomes self-evident that there is a need to get organized and that a schedule would be quite helpful. The degree of need will depend on your memory capacity. However, with 10 or more customers, it's absolutely essential to have a schedule.

Having a schedule makes it easy to keep track of a variety of simple things, such as your customers' names, addresses, telephone numbers, mowing times, and prices. This kind of information is entered on a schedule only once, and it hardly ever changes. Not unless, for example, one of your customers were to move away, in which case you would erase that particular customer from the schedule. As new customers are acquired, the schedule continues to grow, by adding the entries for each new customer.

There are significant advantages to having a schedule; it provides you with simple records of when each customer's lawn had been mowed last, when each customer's lawn is supposed to be mowed next, which customers have paid, and which ones owe money. Thus, you're able to maintain up-to-date information on every customer, always knowing exactly where you stand.

Keeping a schedule is one of the highest levels of maturity for planning and being organized. A schedule, in fact, is indispensable to most people who operate a business.

THE CUSTOMERS

There are, primarily, two different ways of knowing when to mow a customer's lawn. Some customers will always call you a few days or a week in advance of when they want it done. And so you schedule them as necessary when they call.

Other customers, however, prefer to have their lawns mowed on more regular, specific time intervals, such as, on a particular day every week, every 10 days, or on a particular day every other week. It varies, depending on the customer's personal choice and also because some customers' lawns grow faster than others. These people hardly ever call you. They expect to have their grass cut as planned, based on whatever agreement you have with them. So you can plan them in your schedule for as much as three or four weeks in advance.

Occasionally, schedules are subject to change. The main reason is the weather. Due to weather variations, some customers may want their lawn mowed more or less frequently than previously planned. They call and let you know. Then make the appropriate adjustments to their schedules.

WEATHER EFFECTS

Weather conditions can change the rate at which grass will grow. This, in turn, affects the time between mowings. Grass commonly grows faster in the spring than it does in the summer and fall. However, it also grows faster during rainy periods than it does during dry spells. Dry spells slow down the business, and rainy periods speed it up.

Therefore, the intervals between mowings, for all customers, can be affected by the time of the year and also by short-term changes in weather. Now you can begin to better appreciate the need for having a schedule.

It's handy to keep the schedule close by the telephone. This is where it will be most convenient for making scheduling notes while talking to customers. Also, the schedule provides a quick telephone number reference when you need to call a customer. It saves thumbing through a thick telephone directory.

SAMPLE SCHEDULE

Look at the SAMPLE SCHEDULE shown in Figure 24. It shows a simple technique of scheduling that was used for the 11 customers which were given in the examples. The schedule is based on actual recorded data from experience, and it covers the 1981 mowing season. It starts at the end of April and runs to the middle of October, very nearly a six-month period.

Note that the customers' names, addresses, telephone numbers, mowing times, and prices are given in the left-hand column, and the calendar index used for scheduling each customer, on a certain date, runs horizontally across the schedule. The shaded-in areas show the particular dates on which each customer's lawn was mowed. This makes it possible to observe the number of mowings and the interval between mowings for each of the customers over a six-month season. You can see that the lawns were mowed more frequently during the springtime months of May and June than during the other months.

Over the whole season there was a total of 138 mowings for the 11 customers. This is an average of about 12.5 mowings for each customer. Therefore, a customer who pays $10 for each mowing would be worth approximately $125 over a six-month season.

The statistics which may be extracted from the SAMPLE SCHEDULE are interesting. For example, it is possible to determine the variation in the workload through the mowing season.

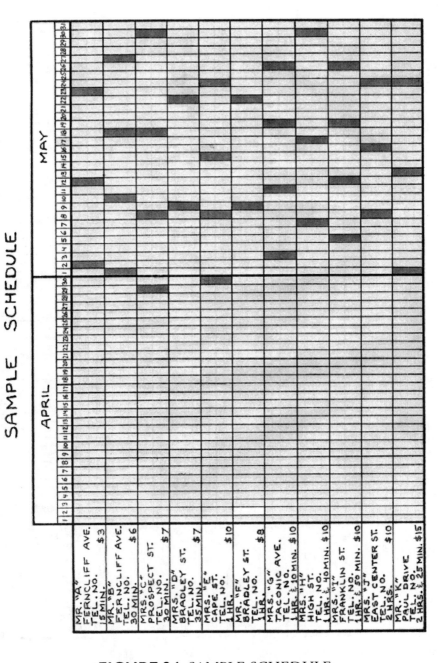

FIGURE 24. SAMPLE SCHEDULE

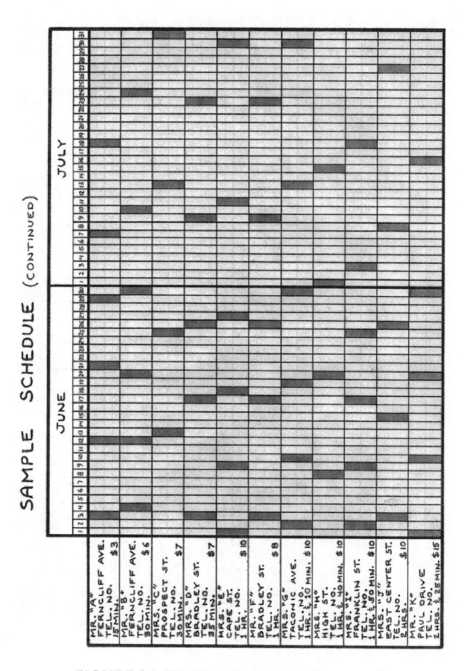

FIGURE 24. SAMPLE SCHEDULE (Continued)

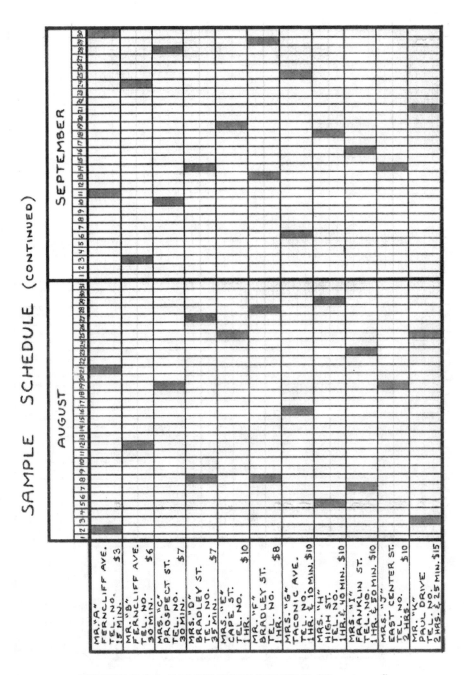

FIGURE 24. SAMPLE SCHEDULE (Continued)

SAMPLE SCHEDULE (CONTINUED)

OCTOBER

The shaded-in areas indicate the dates to show when each customer's lawn was mowed.

Observe that some lawns are mowed more often than other lawns. This is for two reasons. The first being that some customers like to have their lawn mowed more frequently than others. The second being that certain lawns just naturally grow faster than others, demanding more frequent mowings.

So, the time interval between mowings is not the same for all customers.

The schedule shows 1981 mowing-season data.

MR. "A" FERNCLIFF AVE. TEL. NO. 15 MIN. $3
MR. "B" FERNCLIFF AVE. TEL. NO. 30 MIN. $6
MRS. "C" PROSPECT ST. TEL. NO. 30 MIN. $7
MRS. "D" BRADLEY ST. TEL. NO. 35 MIN. $7
MRS. "E" CAPE ST. TEL. NO. 1 HR. $10
MR. "F" BRADLEY ST. TEL. NO. 1 HR. $8
MRS. "G" TACONIC AVE. TEL. NO. 1 HR. & 10 MIN. $10
MRS. "H" HIGH ST. TEL. NO. 1 HR. & 40 MIN. $10
MRS. "I" FRANKLIN ST. TEL. NO. 1 HR. & 50 MIN. $10
MRS. "J" EAST-CENTER ST. TEL. NO. 2 HRS. $10
MR. "K" PAUL DRIVE TEL. NO. 2 HRS. & 25 MIN. $15

FIGURE 24. SAMPLE SCHEDULE (Continued)

This can be done by looking at how the number of mowings per month changes, and also at how the time interval between mowings changes each month.

MOWINGS PER MONTH:

The numbers of mowings during each month were as follows:

April:	2 mowings	(1% of total)
May:	34 mowings	(25% of total)
June:	37 mowings	(27% of total)
July:	21 mowings	(15% of total)
Aug:	17 mowings	(12% of total)
Sept:	16 mowings	(12% of total)
Oct:	11 mowings	(8% of total)
Seasonal Total:	138 mowings	100%

This distribution of the monthly variation in workload is shown in Figure 25. It would apply only if you were to have exactly the same number of customers throughout a mowing season. Therefore, if you were to add on more customers at the beginning of July, as an example, then there would also be a corresponding increase in your workload during July, August, September and October.

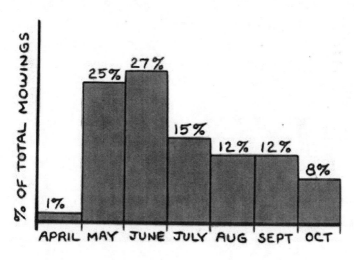

FIGURE 25. Monthly Variation in Workload

It can be seen that the greatest number of mowings occur during May and June; then in July, then in August and September; then October, and then April. Therefore, after June, the number of mowings per month decreases as the mowing season progresses. Surprisingly, about half of all the mowings are done in the two month period of May and June.

TIME BETWEEN MOWINGS

The average time between mowings is an indication of how fast the grass grows. Since grass does grow at different rates during the mowing season, it is of interest to see what effect this has on the workload. The average time between mowings was as follows:

April: not enough data to be applicable
May: about every 10 days between mowings
June: about every 9 days between mowings
July: about every 16 days between mowings
Aug: about every 20 days between mowings
Sept   about every 21 days between mowings
Oct: about every 31 days between mowings

Notice that the average time between mowings gets longer and longer after the month of June. This explains why the number of mowings per month begins to decrease after June. Consequently, the workload also decreases. Therefore, July is a good time to consider adding on more customers, if so desired, to still fill the available work hours that you may have.

Both the average number of mowings per month and the average time between mowings per month were found to be quite typical for three consecutive mowing seasons (1980, 1981, and 1982).

The SAMPLE SCHEDULE has shown the results of when lawns were mowed during an entire mowing season. But, it has not shown the special notations (or symbols) that were used as part of the scheduling process.

SPECIAL NOTATIONS

Special notations are needed during the scheduling process. Various methods of notations can be used. However, the notations which were used are a result of having experimented with different methods, and, therefore, are considered to be about the simplest and most efficient. There are only three notations required for scheduling.

Use an "X" to denote the dates on which you are scheduling, in advance, to mow your customers' lawns. After having mowed the lawns, completely shade in the "X"-marked areas (as shown in the SAMPLE SCHEDULE). This indicates when the lawns were last mowed. If a particular customer didn't pay you, then put a circle around the shaded-in area. This is to remind yourself to collect from the customer.

After collecting, erase the circle. This indicates that the customer has paid.

Any customer who pays immediately after you've finished mowing the lawn (which most of them do), would not have a circle around the shaded-in areas. Consequently, you know that these customers have already paid. Therefore, any shaded-in area without a circle around it indicates that the lawn has been mowed, and the customer has paid.

These three symbols are all that is needed to maintain a complete schedule of your business activity, and they are summarized as follows:

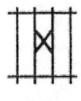 An "X" indicates the scheduled date to mow a particular customer's lawn.

 When shaded-in (covering over the "X"), this indicates that the lawn has been mowed, and the customer has paid.

When shaded-in and encircled, this indicates that the lawn has been mowed, but the customer has not yet paid. (When the customer pays, erase the circle.)

You may want to try a system of notations of your own. Nevertheless, the notations given are suggested for your convenience, and they are also an aid to understanding the scheduling process.

MODE OF TRANSPORTATION

Another consideration associated with scheduling is your mode of transportation. Scheduling considerations can involve traveling time to and from a job, as well as mowing time on the job. If you have a means of rapidly transporting your mower in a truck, station wagon, or automobile trunk, then traveling time is not very significant; that is, within the local areas of a single town. But, if you don't have a means of transportation and plan to walk with the mower, then traveling time becomes a significant consideration.

The average person walks about three miles per hour, which means that accepting a job three miles from your home will take you an hour to walk to the job and an hour to walk back. Of course, this would be rather extreme. Therefore, set a practical limit on the distance you will walk.

For example, if you were to set a limit on mowing all the lawns that you could get only within a one-mile radius of your home, the customers which would be farthest away would require about a 20-minute walk. And all the other, or the majority, of your customers would be even closer. This confines all the customers to within reasonable walking distances.

Restricting the walking distance to within a one-mile radius will allow covering a circular area of 3.14 square miles. This is a large area, and it could include many homes. First try to get all the jobs closest to where you live and then work your way outward to the one-mile limit, as necessary. Keep the customers as close to home as possible so as to minimize the walking distances.

FIGURE 26. *Walking to Mowing Jobs*

(A mower can be easily transported in a small station wagon, as shown in the 1976 Vega, or in the trunk space of medium-sized cars.)

FIGURE 27. *Driving to Mowing Jobs*

If the neighborhood is heavily populated, you may want to consider limiting the walking distance to within just a half-mile radius of home. This would allow covering a circular area of a little more than 75% of a square mile. In this case, the maximum walking time to a job would be only about 10 minutes.

Walking to and from a job can have a certain advantage. It becomes highly visible to many people that you mow lawns. The great majority of neighbors that you pass along the way will eventually see you. This is free advertising. You might even consider putting a simple, removable, cardboard sign on the mower. Name, telephone number, and the word "reliable" is all you need say.

WORKING INTO A SCHEDULE

Working into a schedule of mowing lawns for about 10 to 20 customers is not too difficult if you're in fair physical condition. But, if you consider yourself to be physically out of shape, it will be best to work into your schedule slowly. Start with only a few customers and then expand as you develop your strength. Mowing lawns will build you up physically, both your upper body strength and your legs as well.

So, if your lifestyle has not included any aerobic exercise, such as a lot of walking, or some occasional running, or bicycling, or swimming, or any kind of active sports, then it would be wise to start off with only four or five customers. This shouldn't be too demanding on the legs. And, remember, you don't have to hurry; customers don't care how long it takes to mow their lawn. Take all the breaks you need.

After about a month, you will begin to feel noticeably stronger. Then start adding on more customers.

The lawns in the 11 example jobs which are shown in this book were mowed by John, when he was 15. He was 5' 7" tall and weighed 115 pounds. The following mowing season (during 1982), he was 5' 8" tall, weighed 128 pounds, and was mowing lawns for 20 customers. He could have had many more customers. But at the time, he was already earning enough money. However, two mowing seasons later (in 1984),

SCHEDULE FORM

NAME

STREET

TEL. NO.

MOWING TIME   PRICE

MONTH _____

	1	2	3	4	5	6	7	8	9	10	11	12	13	14	15	16	17	18	19	20	21	22	23	24	25	26	27	28	29	30	31

SCHEDULE FORM

MONTH _____

	1	2	3	4	5	6	7	8	9	10	11	12	13	14	15	16	17	18	19	20	21	22	23	24	25	26	27	28	29	30	31

NAME

STREET

TEL. NO.

MOWING TIME   PRICE

SCHEDULE FORM

MONTH _____

NAME

STREET

TEL. NO.

MOWING TIME   PRICE

	1	2	3	4	5	6	7	8	9	10	11	12	13	14	15	16	17	18	19	20	21	22	23	24	25	26	27	28	29	30	31

SCHEDULE FORM

MONTH _____

NAME						
STREET						
TEL. NO.						
MOWING TIME	PRICE					

	1	2	3	4	5	6	7	8	9	10	11	12	13	14	15	16	17	18	19	20	21	22	23	24	25	26	27	28	29	30	31

SCHEDULE FORM

NAME

STREET

TEL. NO.

MOWING TIME   PRICE

MONTH

1	2	3	4	5	6	7	8	9	10	11	12	13	14	15	16	17	18	19	20	21	22	23	24	25	26	27	28	29	30	31

SCHEDULE FORM

	MONTH _____

	1	2	3	4	5	6	7	8	9	10	11	12	13	14	15	16	17	18	19	20	21	22	23	24	25	26	27	28	29	30	31

NAME _____

STREET _____

TEL. NO. _____

MOWING TIME _____ PRICE _____

SCHEDULE FORM

MONTH

1	2	3	4	5	6	7	8	9	10	11	12	13	14	15	16	17	18	19	20	21	22	23	24	25	26	27	28	29	30	31

NAME

STREET

TEL. NO.

MOWING TIME   PRICE

SCHEDULE FORM

MONTH _____

	NAME	STREET	TEL. NO.	MOWING TIME	PRICE
1					
2					
3					
4					
5					
6					
7					
8					
9					
10					
11					
12					
13					
14					
15					
16					
17					
18					
19					
20					
21					
22					
23					
24					
25					
26					
27					
28					
29					
30					
31					

SCHEDULE FORM

NAME					
STREET					
TEL. NO.					
MOWING TIME	PRICE				

MONTH

	1	2	3	4	5	6	7	8	9	10	11	12	13	14	15	16	17	18	19	20	21	22	23	24	25	26	27	28	29	30	31

SCHEDULE FORM

MONTH

	1	2	3	4	5	6	7	8	9	10	11	12	13	14	15	16	17	18	19	20	21	22	23	24	25	26	27	28	29	30	31

NAME

STREET

TEL. NO.

MOWING TIME   PRICE

SCHEDULE FORM

CHAPTER 6

SAFETY

Consider the underlying theme of "safety first". This theme is just as appropriate for operating a power mower as it is for operating any other kind of powered equipment. Take the automobile, for example. We're all well aware that driving an automobile without exercising safety precautions can be quite hazardous. Yet, some people still drive recklessly and habitually get into accidents. But, there are also millions of people who drive many miles every day and don't have an accident. This is because they are careful, considerate, and obey rules of the road. These people operate their automobiles with safety in mind. You should do likewise when operating a power mower.

Obviously, collision with another mower is unlikely to happen. So, in this one particular respect, there is much less risk than when being out on the road driving an automobile. There is also the advantage of having more independent control over the possible hazardous occurrences that can be associated with operating a power mower. First of all, you're on your own two feet, walking behind the mower. Secondly, you're moving rather slowly. And thirdly, there isn't any congested, interfering traffic to contend with on the lawn.

However, you're still assuming some risks. The risks are of a different nature. For this reason, there are a number of rules of safety that should be observed when using a power mower. These rules can be classified into several different categories. They include safety associated with **general operating conditions**; safety associated with making any **adjustments, inspections and repairs**; safety associated with certain **attachments** on the mower; safety associated with **storage** of the mower; safety associated with handling **gasoline**; safety associated with maintaining proper oil levels; and, safety associated with **mowing procedures.**

GENERAL OPERATING CONDITIONS

Rules of safety for general operation of a mower should be taken just as seriously as you would take the rules for operating an automobile. It's important to become familiar with, and obey, these rules faithfully.

They are listed as follows:

- Read the owner's manual carefully and refer to it often. It will show simple illustrations of mower parts, basic operating instructions, and minor maintenance procedures.

- Properly maintain the mower by following the manufacturer's instructions.

- Know the controls and how to stop the mower quickly.

- Avoid wearing any loose-fitting clothing that could possibly get caught in the mower equipment.

- Always wear substantial footwear such as rough-soled, heavy duty shoes; never wear open sandals.

- Mow only in daylight or in good artificial light.

- Don't operate mower in wet grass or where foot traction is unsure.

- Don't allow children lacking in maturity, experience, and physical strength to operate the mower.

- Look over the lawn and remove any loose items such as sticks, wires, bones, stones or other foreign objects before mowing.

- If there are any firmly implanted stone boundary markers or protruding pipes, they should be temporarily marked by placing a clearly visible item over them. This will flag your attention when mowing nearby this type of hidden object. A quick and simple method of marking is to push a stick vertically into the lawn next to these obstructions. (The customer usually knows exactly where they're located and will show you.)

- Don't run the mower over loose objects.

- Keep everyone away, especially small children, when operating the mower.

- Wear ear plugs and safety glasses.

- Don't stand near the discharge opening when starting the engine or while the mower is in operation.

- Don't discharge grass towards people or into an area where a thrown object might result in a personal injury or property damage.

- Run the engine at its lowest speed that cuts properly. This will reduce the potential hazard from a thrown object. (Also, the mower will wear more slowly and give a longer service life.)

- Don't change the engine governor settings in any way or tamper with parts that may increase the governed speed.

- Keep a firm hold on the handle and walk. Never run.

- Push, don't pull, the mower.

- Don't place hands or feet near the mower housing when the engine is running.

- Always keep hands and feet clear of rotating parts.

- Keep the engine free of an accumulation of grass or excess grease and oil.

- Stop the engine before taking the mower off the lawn to keep the rotating blade from hitting the edge of walkways, driveways, or roadways.

- Stop the engine when leaving the mower. Make certain the blade and all moving parts have stopped.

As of June 30, 1982, all new power mowers are required to have a control that will automatically stop the blades on all walk-behind models within three seconds after the handle is released. The Consumer Product Safety Commission imposed this built-in safety standard on all lawn mower manufacturers. The law allows for mowers without the feature to be sold only if they were already in stock before June 30, 1982.

ADJUSTMENTS, INSPECTIONS, AND REPAIRS

As a hard-and-fast rule, do not unclog the discharge opening, clean the mower housing, and make any inspections, adjustments, or repairs without first stopping the engine and then removing the spark plug wire from the spark plug. Removing the spark plug wire prevents unexpected, or accidental, starting of the engine. (The spark plug wire is held on by a clip which is easily and quickly removable by hand, without need of a tool.)

There is one exception for leaving the engine running during an adjustment. This is when adjusting the carburetor. It must be left running to listen for smooth engine performance while the carburetor adjustment is being made. Other rules are as follows:

- Never make a wheel height adjustment while the engine is running.

- Keep all nuts, bolts, and screws tight to be certain the mower is in safe operating condition.

- Check the blade adapter bolt and engine mounting bolts at frequent intervals for proper tightness.

- If you should strike a foreign object, stop the engine and remove the spark plug wire. Thoroughly inspect the mower for damage. If damaged, have the mower repaired before restarting.

- If the mower starts to vibrate, stop the engine and remove the spark plug wire. Check for cause of vibration. Vibration is generally a warning of trouble.

There are a few principal reasons that can cause vibration to occur. The engine mounting bolts are loose or the blade is either loose, bent, or unbalanced. Another possible reason is that the shaft (which rotates the blade) has been bent. This can happen if you hit a solid, foreign object quite hard.

If you bend the shaft, this will require major repair work, which leads to another rule:

> **Do not attempt to make any major engine repairs unless you have the proper tools and a thorough knowledge of internal combustion engine repair procedures. You could either injure yourself or ruin the mower. Bring major repair work to your local lawn mower serviceman.**

ATTACHMENTS

Attachments are additional items which are connected to the mower. They consist of such things as a chute deflector, exhaust deflector, grass catcher, spark arrester, and guards. The attachments provide some form of protection in one respect or another. Safety rules associated with attachments are as follows:

- Don't operate the mower without attachments or safety protective devices in place.

- Don't operate the mower if it is equipped with a grass catcher unless an exhaust deflector has been installed. (The exhaust deflector prevents grass from coming in contact with the hot exhaust system and causing a fire hazard.)

- Always stop the engine and remove the spark plug wire from the spark plug before attaching or removing a grass catcher, if the mower is so equipped.

- Ensure that the chute deflector is always over the top of the chute so as to deflect thrown grass toward the ground, when a grass catcher is not being used.

- Don't operate the mower without a muffler or tamper with the exhaust system. (A damaged exhaust system or lack of using a muffler can be a fire hazard.)

- Don't operate the mower on any forest covered, brush covered, field covered or unimproved land without the muffler being equipped with a spark arrestor. Otherwise, the mower creates a fire hazard. (The spark arrester is not required for mowing ordinary lawns.)

- Never touch the muffler or exhaust system while the engine is running or right after it has been running. (The exhaust system and muffler system get very hot.)

STORAGE

Safety associated with storage of a mower is important because, while a mower is in storage, flammable gasoline fumes can be released and accumulated. And, running a mower inside of an enclosed area will cause toxic fumes to build up. So:

- Don't store the mower indoors or inside an unventilated enclosure where gasoline fumes may accumulate or reach an open flame or spark.

- Don't run the engine in an enclosed area. Exhaust gases contain carbon monoxide which is a colorless, odorless and deadly poisonous gas.

- Don't store a gasoline container near an open flame or any kind of spark exposure.

- Always ensure that the cover on a gasoline container is tight enough to prevent the release and accumulation of fumes, particularly when stored in an enclosed area.

Be certain to provide some ventilation if the mower is to be stored in an enclosed area. If it's difficult or impractical for you to provide sufficient ventilation, then leave the mower outside. Use plastic or some other kind of waterproof cover for rust protection from the rain. And, always allow the engine to cool before covering the mower, or before storing the mower in an enclosed area,

GASOLINE

Have respect for gasoline. Treat, it with care. Always be aware that when it's not handled with care, it can be a safety hazard. Therefore:

- Don't smoke while handling gasoline. The fumes are highly flammable.

- Use only a container that is specifically made for handling gasoline. These containers are easily recognized because they say "for gasoline" or just "gasoline" on the container, usually in large letters.

- Do not store, spill, or use gasoline near an open flame or near devices such as a stove, furnace, or water heater which use a tiny flame for a pilot light, or near devices that can create a spark.

- If gasoline is accidentally spilled, move the mower away from the area of the spill and avoid creating any source of ignition until gasoline vapors have dissipated.

- Fill the gasoline tank outdoors or only in well-ventilated areas.

- Wipe off any spills on the mower before starting the engine.

- Don't fuel the engine while it is running or when the engine is hot. Wait for the engine to cool before refilling the tank.

OIL

It is a good safety practice to check for the proper quantity of oil before starting the engine. Two problems can arise if the mower is operated without a sufficient amount of oil: One, an unlubricated engine will overheat, causing a fire hazard. Two, this can also cause rapid wearing which will ruin internal engine parts.

MOWING PROCEDURES

Slopes should be cut only in a lengthwise direction (Figure 28). Do not mow slopes by walking the mower straight up or straight down (Figure 29). There is danger of slipping or losing your footing. Excessively steep slopes, or wherever there is uncertainty of good footing, should be avoided altogether.

Don't mow in wet grass. It's slippery. Wait until the grass is *dry*.

For your initial cutting, first mow only on level ground. Get a good feel for handling the mower. Then proceed to mow the slopes. On level ground, cut long straight strips, overlapping each strip slightly. When mowing around trees, posts, and other obstructions, bring the left side of the mower up close, following the contour of the object. The left side of the mower is the opposite side of the discharge chute.

Thick grass is best cut by mowing such that the discharge chute is facing outward, starting at the extreme outside border of the lawn and working toward the center. By following this procedure, the cutting blade is not forced to pick up heavy clippings from each of the previous rounds of cutting; therefore, requiring less engine power and resulting in a more even cut. Essentially, this is accomplished by mowing in a counter-clockwise direction.

There are adjustable settings for the height of cut. It's best to regularly set the mower so as to cut the grass a bit long rather than cutting it too short. This applies particularly in hot weather when blades of grass should be left tall enough to at least provide sufficient shade for the grass roots. Otherwise, the sun can dry the soil so quickly that the grass may turn brown, and possibly die. (Some customers' lawns will turn brown in certain areas every summer which are for reasons beyond your control, such as poor soil conditions or disease.)

John Deere & Company recommends that cool-season grasses, found in the northern part of the country, be mowed to a height of 2 to 2 1/2 inches and cut again after the lawn grows an inch. Warm-Season grasses in southern areas should be cut to a height of 1 to 2 inches and removed when they reach 1 1/2 to 2 1/2 inches.

Keep the blade reasonably sharp enough to ensure a good clean cut. A dull blade can result in splitting or bruising the grass ends and cause some temporary browning of the freshly cut area.

Follow all the basic rules of safety for a long, continual, successful operation with your mower.

DISCLAIMER

It is common knowledge that injuries can occur with all types of powered equipment. Lawn mowers are no exception. This is why you were made well aware of the need to exercise safety. Safety is your responsibility. The author, publisher and marketer of this book accept no responsibility in the event that an injury should occur and, therefore, disclaim all liability for any personal injuries or material damages.

FIGURE 28. Correct Procedure for Mowing Slopes

FIGURE 29. Incorrect Procedure for Mowing Slopes

Chapter 7

MAINTENANCE

Maintenance is a separate study in itself. And then, it's only through extensive experience that one eventually becomes expert at all aspects of maintenance. Therefore, it will be best if you rely on a mower repairman to make any kind of involved repairs. There are, however, some simple types of maintenance that you can do yourself.

Maintenance is divided into two different levels of ability: minor maintenance and major maintenance. Minor maintenance consists of doing things that require very little skill, such as cleaning, lubricating, and making simple adjustments. It also includes making relatively easy repairs, such as replacing a wheel, changing a spark plug, or sharpening the blade. This is the type of maintenance that you can consider doing yourself.

Major maintenance work primarily consists of making very involved and intricate repairs to the engine, carburetor, and controlling mechanisms. Attempting to correct these types of problems, when you don't know what you're doing, can lead to frustration, poor results, and higher than necessary cost for final repairs. Furthermore, major maintenance repairs can be dangerous to those who do not have a clear understanding of detailed procedures.

So, it's best to envision yourself primarily in terms of operating the mower, using your time productively to earn money, rather than getting bogged down with major maintenance work. Major repairs should not be attempted unless you have the proper tools and a thorough knowledge of repair procedures. Your nearest service center for mower repairs is listed in the yellow pages of the telephone directory either under "Engines, Gasoline", "Gasoline Engines", or "Lawn Mowers".

When you purchase a mower, you'll get an Owner's Manual (sometimes called an Owner's Handbook) with it. The manual will show basic operating instructions along with some illustrations and simple procedures for doing minor maintenance work. The manual will not contain information on major maintenance; it is usually suggested in the manual that this type of work be done only by an authorized manufacturer's dealer or a mower repairman.

MAJOR MAINTENANCE

For those who are mechanically talented and eager to do their own major maintenance work, there are several books that have been written on the subject. Many of these books, however, generally cover the theory, operation, and maintenance of all kinds of engines as a broad subject, and do not treat lawn mowers in detail as a dedicated subject. Four books that specifically cover lawn mowers are suggested as follows:

1. Weissler, Paul., "Small Gas Engines: How to Repair and Maintain Them", 1991. Times Mirror Magazines, Inc., Book Division, 2 Park Avenue, New York, NY, 10016.

    (This is a fully illustrated guide to care and repair of small gas engines. The book concentrates entirely on chain saws, snow blowers, and lawn mowers. You should be able to get this book at the library. If not, then ask the librarian to borrow it on a loan basis from another library. This isn't unusual; it's done quite frequently.)

2. "Services and Repair Instructions", Briggs and Stratton Corp., Milwaukee, Wisconsin.

    (This illustrated book includes theories of operation, common specifications, and detailed information covering the adjustment, tune-up, and repair procedures for 2 through 16 horsepower single cylinder engines for lawn mowers. Briggs and Stratton Corporation manufacture many of the engines that are used for lawn mowers.

    The book can be purchased from any authorized Briggs and Stratton service center. Look for a service center in your area in the yellow pages of the telephone directory. If the service center does not have the book in stock, the Service Manager can order it for you.)

3. "Walking Behind Lawn Mower Service Manual", 1991. Intertec Publishing Corp., 9800 Metcalf Ave., Shawnee Mission, KS 66212.

    (This is a complete guide for the care and repair of walk-behind, push-type lawn mowers. There are many enlarged views that show step-by-step maintenance instructions. The book covers various makes of engines that are used on many lawn mowers, which include Lawn Boy, Jacobsen, Craftsman, Clinton, Tecumseh, and Briggs and Stratton.)

4. "Riding Lawn Mower Service Manual", 1993. Intertec Publishing Corp., 9800 Metcalf Ave., Shawnee Mission, KS 66212-2215.

    (This book contains hundreds of detailed photographs and illustrations that show instructions from disassembly to assembly. It covers a large variety of riding mowers that are made by many different manufacturers, which include: Allis-Chalmers, AMF, Columbia, FMC-Bolens, John Deere, Dixon XTR, Dynamark, Gilson,

Homelite, International Harvester, Jacobsen, Lawn Boy, Massey-Ferguson, MTD, Murray, Roper, Simplicity, Snapper, Wheel Horse, and White.)

Before acquiring one of the books listed above, check with a local dealer who sells your make of lawn mower. The dealer should be able to inform you as to whether or not the manufacturer sells a manual that covers major maintenance for your particular lawn mower. If so, the dealer may have the book in stock. If not, he can order it for you. Therefore, the first place to check for a manual is with the dealer.

Another source of knowledge can be through your local school system. Many vocational schools teach a course on small engine repair. Also, some high schools offer special courses on small engine repair that are taught nights and/or during the summer sessions. Most of the in-depth knowledge is associated with an understanding of the engine.

The need for major maintenance can actually be avoided to a significant degree. By operating a mower properly and performing minor maintenance requirements faithfully, in accordance with instructions given in your Owner's Manual, the need for major maintenance will be considerably reduced. This can hold true up to the point where the mower begins to reach the end of its operating life. Then, the decision to either have a significant amount of major maintenance work done or buy a new mower is inevitable.

LIFE OF A MOWER

The life of a mower will depend on how well it is treated by the operator and how frequently it is used. Mistreatment and a lack of minor maintenance will shorten its life. Giving it proper care will extend the life. Also, there is something very simple that can be done to greatly extend the life of a mower:

If your mower is equipped with an engine variable-speed control lever, always operate the engine at the slowest speed that cuts properly. Any additional, unnecessary speed will cause needless engine wear. Don't make the engine go through more operating cycles than necessary. This is a mistake that is very often made by many people when operating their lawn mowers.

The inexpensive, self-push, rotary mower that had been used for the 11 example jobs was also used for other mowing jobs, which were not given in the examples. (These other mowing jobs consisted of some larger, less profitable house lots; and, as a result of experience, they were not recommended in the class of small lawns.) All told, the mower had gone through an estimated 375 mowings of small lawns, averaging about a quarter-acre in size. This was over a period of two six-month mowing seasons.

The mower reached the end of its life shortly after the beginning of the third mowing season. That is, it needed a major overhaul, which was nearly as expensive as buying a new mower. Therefore, the mower did the equivalent of serving about 15 customers (with small lawns) for a little more than two mowing seasons. This would also be equivalent to serving either 30 customers for one six-month mowing season or serving 10 customers for three six-month mowing seasons.

SPARE MOWER

One way of avoiding a temporary interruption of business, should your mower require major repairs, is to have a spare mower. With two mowers, you'll always have some back-up in the event that one is not operating. The additional one could be purchased as a used mower.

It's usually not very difficult to buy a good-running, second-hand mower. There are people who sell their homes to move into an apartment and, therefore, sell their lawn mower. Sometimes people who are moving far away will sell many of their belongings, including their mower. Second-hand mowers normally sell for about a third of the price of a new one. Prices vary to some extent depending on age and condition. There are many sources for buying used mowers. Look in the classified-ad sections of newspapers. Go to garage sales. Go to tag sales. Ask a mower repairman to let you know when he has a used mower to sell, or, run your own ad: "Looking for used mower in good running condition."

MINOR MAINTENANCE

Because the designs of mowers are somewhat different from one manufacturer to another, the minor maintenance requirements can also vary to some degree. What's more, the minor maintenance requirements can vary between different models made by the same manufacturer. Therefore, minor maintenance procedures and illustrations are not covered here. Use your Owner's Manual. The manual will contain all the necessary information that you will need, and it will apply uniquely to the manufacturer's specifications for the particular model of mower that you purchase.

The manual will give the procedures for overall operation, adjustments, and minor maintenance. Many manufacturers also include a trouble-shooting list so that you are able to isolate the cause of a problem. A typical Owner's Manual will give a set of procedures that cover such things as:

> Operation
> Lubrication
> Fueling
> Cleaning
> Blade Care
> Air Filter Care
> Spark Plug Care
> Wheel Adjustments
> Carburetor Adjustments
> Throttle Control Adjustments
> Replacement of Minor Parts

The instructions are sufficiently clear to permit an average owner to understand the basic operating procedures, simple adjustments, and minor maintenance requirements.

SPECIAL EMPHASIS

In addition to the information that will be given in your Owner's Manual, there are certain areas of interest which are worth emphasizing. These are relatively simple, yet significant concerns that directly relate to extending the life of a mower. They include: avoid hitting solid objects;

make occasional checks to ensure that all nuts, screws, and bolts are kept properly tightened; be certain that all working parts are always well lubricated; keep the engine clean from an accumulation of dirt and debris; and, maintain a reasonably sharp blade at all times. Also, if the mower is equipped with an engine variable-speed-control lever, ensure that the engine is operated at its slowest speed that cuts properly.

SOLID OBJECTS

Under normal operating conditions, the blade of a rotary mower is rotating somewhere between 1800 and 3600 revolutions per minute, depending on the engine speed setting. There's a considerable amount of momentum in the spinning blade. If it were to hit a large protruding root of a big tree, a sturdy iron-pipe boundary marker, or a concrete curb, the blade would come to a jolting halt. One great thud!

The impact could cause any one of three things to happen. First, if you're lucky, the only damage that would occur is that the blade would either bend or break. This type of repair would require just minor maintenance to the extent of replacing the blade. Second, because the blade is firmly attached to a shaft, it's also possible that the shaft could bend. A bent shaft must either be perfectly straightened or replaced (usually replaced). This requires major maintenance work and should be done by a mower repairman. Since the shaft is linked to, and driven by, the engine, the third and worst possible thing that can go wrong is to have the impact reflect damage into the engine. It is possible to seriously damage internal engine parts. This, too, requires major maintenance work and should be done by a mower repairman. Therefore, avoid hitting solid objects.

NUTS, SCREWS AND BOLTS

There are vibrations associated with the normal operation of a power mower. This is inherent in all engines. Vibrations can occasionally cause a nut, screw, or bolt to become loosened. It then becomes possible to lose one of these minor parts, which will consequently cause an adverse effect on the mower. Once lost, it's very difficult to find a missing nut, screw, or bolt, particularly if lost in the grass.

Therefore, eliminate the possibility of losing any minor parts. Make occasional inspections. Check to see that all nuts, screws, and bolts are securely fastened. Do this about every 20 hours of operation. It's a simple, quick inspection that can be done in just a few minutes.

LUBRICATION

Mechanically moving parts need to be regularly lubricated. Lubricants provide a durable, slippery coating that removes nearly all friction and considerably reduces wear. This is what allows an engine and its associated mechanisms to perform with smooth, long-lasting operation. Nothing will shorten the life of a mower faster than a lack of proper lubrication.

Three main areas for lubrication are the engine, its controlling mechanisms, and the mower wheels. Most critical is the engine. Your Owner's Manual will give the manufacturer's recommendation for oiling the engine of the particular model mower that you purchase. Adhere to the recommendations faithfully. Typically, engine oil needs to be changed about every 25 hours of operation. Capacity is usually a little more than one pint. Oil needs to be changed because it gets dirty or grimy from tiny, abrasive particles that collect in the oil. When dirty, the quality of lubrication diminishes, and there is less protection against wear.

Those who own mowers that are equipped with an engine variable-speed-control lever often overlook the need to oil this control mechanism. (See Figure 30.) It's used when starting and stopping the engine and also for controlling the engine speed. It consists of a hand-operated lever (which is mounted on the handle of the mower) and a control cable (which connects the lever to the engine). The operator manually positions the lever as desired.

Positioning the lever causes a long, steel wire to move within the control cable. The wire moves by sliding through a center opening, or tunnel, inside of the cable. Since the cable and its internal sliding wire are both usually made of steel, they are subject to rusting and can "freeze up". Therefore, the cable should always be kept oiled. Oil it about once a month. This also applies to any other, similar type of control cables that may, or may not, be on your model of mower.

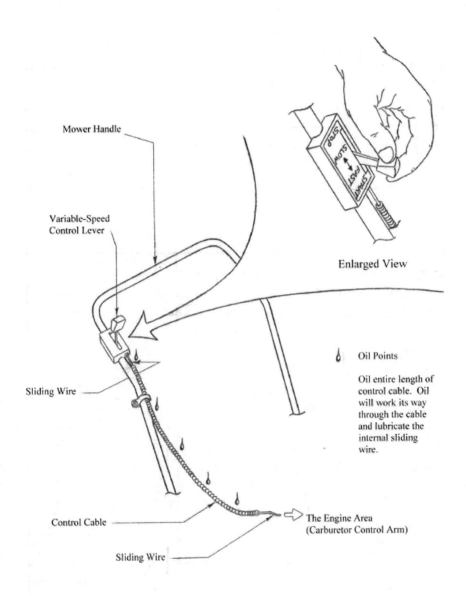

Mower Handle

Variable-Speed
Control Lever

Enlarged View

Sliding Wire

Oil Points

Oil entire length of
control cable. Oil
will work its way
through the cable
and lubricate the
internal sliding
wire.

Control Cable

The Engine Area
(Carburetor Control Arm)

Sliding Wire

FIGURE 30. Variable-Speed-Control Mechanism

Small linkages and little lever arms associated with the carburetor should also be lubricated; doing this once a month is usually sufficient.

A frequently neglected area for lubrication is the wheels. Few people oil them as often as necessary. They are quickly subject to lubrication dry-out and rapid wearing. This is why wheels are sometimes the first items that need to be replaced. To ensure maximum performance and prolong the life of your mower, frequently lubricate the wheel bearings and/or axles with grease or engine oil. Do it after every eight hours of operation. Even more often, if desired. It should be done frequently enough to keep an oily, wet look on the axles.

CLEANING

Engines are designed to operate within a certain temperature range. If allowed to get too hot, they become less efficient and when too hot, the internal engine parts begin to wear out much more quickly than under normal operating temperature conditions. Should the engine ever start to smoke - usually a faint bluish color - this is a clear indication that it's overheated. Don't operate under these conditions. The engine can "burn out".

Overheating will occur if the engine does not have enough oil. But overheating can also be caused as a result of the engine being very dirty. So keep the engine clean. A stiff brush will do the job. Make sure that the cooling fins on the cylinder are not plugged with grass, dirt, or other debris. Free circulation of air around the cylinder and between the cooling fins is essential for proper engine performance and long life.

It's normally over a period of many mowings that a build-up of debris will begin to collect on the engine. So, frequent cleaning is not usually required. When you see a build-up, that's the time to clean it.

Another area for cleaning is the underside of the mower housing. It is necessary to keep the underside of the mower clean and free from grass build-up to maintain cutting efficiency. Clean this area after each mowing. When cutting heavy, moist grass, the underside will have to be cleaned more frequently.

BLADE CARE

Overheating of the engine can also be caused by mowing through thick, heavy grass with a very dull blade. A dull blade reduces cutting efficiency. This makes the engine overwork beyond normal conditions, and, therefore, can cause it to overheat. So the blade should be kept reasonably sharp. It can be removed and sharpened in a vice with a file.

After sharpening, always make sure that the blade is well balanced. The blade is checked for balance at its center point, where there is a large hole in the middle of the blade. Insert half the length of a screw-driver through the hole. It will fit through the hole loosely. Hold both the screwdriver and blade in a horizontal position. Then, while firmly holding the screwdriver, let go of the blade. Allow it to freely rest, hori-zontally, on the shank of the screwdriver.

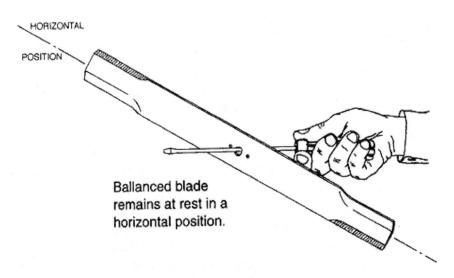

HORIZONTAL

POSITION

Ballanced blade
remains at rest in a
horizontal position.

FIGURE 31. Balanced Blade

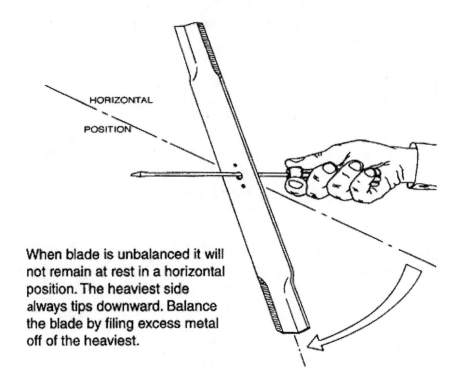

HORIZONTAL

POSITION

When blade is unbalanced it will not remain at rest in a horizontal position. The heaviest side always tips downward. Balance the blade by filing excess metal off of the heaviest.

FIGURE 32. Unbalanced Blade

If the blade remains in a horizontal position it is balanced (See Figure 31). If it does not remain in a horizontal position and begins to slowly turn, of its own accord, it is out of balance. The heaviest side will tip downward (See Figure 32). Balance the blade by filing some metal off of the heaviest side. File excess metal off of any area other than the cutting edge. Then, check for balance again and repeat filing if necessary until the blade comes into balance.

It's very important that the blade be balanced. An unbalanced blade will cause the entire mower to vibrate vigorously and thereby greatly shorten the life of the mower.

There is a way to make the blade hold a sharp edge longer than normal, and, hence, last much longer between sharpening. To do this, you have to harden the steel along the cutting edges. Hardening is done by a heating and cooling process. Only one end of the blade is done at a time, as follows:

Remove the blade from the mower. Then, with a torch, heat only the cutting-edge portion of the blade. Heat it until there is a faint, dull red glow in the thin metal edge. Next, immediately immerse the blade in a bucket of cold water. It will sizzle and harden as it quickly cools down. Repeat this process of heating and cooling about three times. When one end of the blade is done, then do the other end.

If a torch is not available, as an alternate choice, use one of the heating elements on top of a kitchen electric stove. Turn it on "high" and lay only the sharpened portion of the blade directly on the burner. This will heat the blade's sharpened edge to a red glow, like the color of the burner unit itself. The blade will get hot enough for hardening in the same manner as was described for using a torch.

Altogether, it takes about 15 minutes to harden the cutting edges of a blade. This will make the blade hold a reasonably sharp edge for at least twice as long as usual. This will also appreciably extend the life of the blade.

The main purpose for this chapter was to convey only an awareness and an appreciation for the need to give proper attention to minor maintenance requirements. It was also for the purpose of providing some special tips on how to avoid the need for major maintenance and how to prolong the life of a mower. Therefore, this chapter is not a substitute for the overall minor maintenance requirements that will be given in your Owner's Manual.

CHAPTER 8

KEYS TO SUCCESS

There are certain aspects of the mowing business that deserve special consideration. They consist of the most important things that you should do to succeed in making big money mowing small lawns. They are therefore the keys to success. You should:

- Own a mower

- Treat the mower with care

- Specialize in mowing work

- Mow only small lawns

- Avoid mowing steep slopes

- Observe the rules of safety

- Advertise using business cards

- Keep a schedule

- Estimate the amount of mowing work

- Use the PRICE ESTIMATING TABLES

- Be reliable

Each of these keys to success is worth a brief, review. Reviewing them will require: one, relating back to the most significant elements of information that have been covered in the previous chapters and, two, summarizing this information as it applies to each of the keys to success. In doing this, a brief review of the keys to success will also serve as an overall summary of the business.

OWN A MOWER

By having your own mower, there is a good chance of easily doubling and almost tripling the number of customers that you can get. And customers are willing to pay you more money when you provide the mower. So you get more work, and you make more money.

Use an inexpensive, self-push, rotary mower. One that is small and lightweight. It's an easy type of mower to operate, maneuver, and transport between jobs. It also has a minimal number of mechanical parts that are subject to failure. And you can do a considerable amount of mowing work without tiring.

TREAT MOWER WITH CARE

All major maintenance on a mower should be done by a mower repairman. You can and you should do the minor maintenance yourself. Do it regularly in accordance with the procedures given in your Owner's Manual. The need for major maintenance can be avoided to a significant degree by faithfully performing the minor maintenance requirements.

The life of a mower will depend on how well you treat it. Therefore, treat your mower with care. If it is equipped with a variable-speed-control lever, always operate the engine at the slowest speed that cuts properly. Keep the variable-speed-control mechanism, the engine, the wheels, and other moving parts well oiled. Keep a sharp, balanced blade. Avoid hitting solid objects. And, make occasional checks to ensure that nuts, screws, and bolts are kept tight.

SPECIALIZE IN MOWING

Specialize in mowing lawns. Odd jobs such as weeding gardens, washing windows, and painting fences do not pay as well as mowing services. Although some of your customers are apt to offer you these additional kinds of odd jobs, they are not inclined to pay as well for this type of work. They usually want to pay only by the hour at about the minimum-wage level. Your greatest profits will come from specializing in mowing.

MOW SMALL LAWNS

Try to get as many of the smallest lawns as you can. These are the properties of less than a quarter-acre in size that require an hour or less of mowing time. They are the most profitable. Earnings for these lots are about three and a half times the minimum wage rate of pay. Some pay more.

The least profitable jobs you should accept are those that are nearly 0.40 acres. These lots require approximately three hours of mowing time. They pay at a rate that is a little less than double the minimum wage.

Don't accept mowing jobs on properties that are larger than 0.40 acres. This is the cut-off point. These lots are too large. They cause considerable wear on a small, rotary mower. And, properties of this size are not profitable unless you were to invest in a much more expensive mower.

AVOID STEEP SLOPES

Avoid taking jobs on properties with steep slopes. These kinds of mowing jobs can be dangerous. You can lose your footing while mowing. They are also tough jobs that require much more work than usual.

And, customers who own steep-sloped properties don't seem to want to pay for the extra work. So, as a rule, it's best to avoid steep-sloped jobs.

OBSERVE RULES OF SAFETY

Always exercise safety with a power mower. Observe the rules that were given for general operating conditions and for making adjustments, inspections, and repairs. Also, observe the rules of safety that are associated with certain attachments on a mower, with the storage of a mower, with mowing slopes and with handling gasoline. Follow all the basic rules of safety.

ADVERTISE USING BUSINESS CARDS

You will have to advertise to get jobs. Use business cards. Distribute the cards to homeowners. Homeowners will provide the best response for getting jobs in a short period of time. They also have a tendency to be the highest paying customers. Therefore, start off by concentrating on the homeowner market.

You may also consider advertising in a shopping guide. If you advertise in a shopping guide in addition to distributing business cards, this will be the quickest way to get customers.

There will be a difference in response to your advertising depending on the time of year that you advertise. You can advertise any time during the mowing season. But the best time to advertise will be just before the mowing season starts. And, during the first month of the mowing season is also an exceptionally good time to advertise.

KEEP A SCHEDULE

If you have more than five customers, consider having a schedule. If you have 10 or more customers, you must have a schedule. Having a schedule is what makes it easy to keep track of your customers' names, addresses, telephone numbers, mowing times, and prices; when each customer's lawn was last mowed; when each customer's lawn is supposed to be mowed the next time; which customers have paid; and which ones owe money.

A schedule is also convenient for keeping track of your total income. This eliminates the need for bookkeeping. Therefore, you should keep a schedule. The schedule forms provided will help you in getting started.

ESTIMATE THE WORK

When first starting off in the business, you should get an estimate of the size of a house lot or the mowing time. If the customer cannot tell you, then you have a choice of applying any one of three methods that were given: the Equivalent-Square Method, the Acreage Matrix Method, or the Acreage-Equation Method. Whichever method you select, it will be necessary to pace the length and width dimensions of the lot. This can be done in a few minutes. At most, it takes about five minutes to estimate a job. And, estimating is done only once for each customer. This is when you get a call to go look·at a job and quote a price for doing the work.

USE THE PRICE ESTIMATING TABLES

After you have estimated the lot size and mowing time, use the PRICE ESTIMATING TABLES as price guidelines. Use the table that applies to the current minimum wage. If you should find it necessary to make an adjustment in the prices for your area, change the prices. An easy way of changing prices is to disregard the particular table that applies to the current minimum wage and select any other table that best fits your price experience. The PRICE ESTIMATING TABLES can be used quite flexibly in this respect.

Detailed estimating is necessary when you're first getting started in the mowing business. However, after having mowed many properties, you will be able to readily estimate the size of a house lot, the mowing time, and the right price just by observation. This comes with experience, probably about the time that you will have gotten half way through your first mowing season.

When you have determined the price that you're going to charge a customer, be tactful in the way that you state the price. Don't state your price until the customer asks how much it will cost. Wait for them to ask. They all do. They'll ask, "What is your price?" or "How much do you charge?" or "How much?" Then, state the price by answering their question with a question. Ask, "How about $15?" (or whatever the price happens to be). This is a comfortable situation that allows the customer to either agree or disagree. And, with this approach, most customers do agree.

This was found to be the best way to state the price. It is a way of giving the customer some courtesy on the decision in the price. This approach is quite acceptable to just about all customers.

Occasionally, there will be a customer who does not agree with your suggested price. This is when you will have to drop the price a few dollars if you still want the job. Or, refuse the job on the basis that you must stay within your price range (which is the highest price that the majority of customers are willing to pay).

BE RELIABLE

Be reliable enough to cut the grass regularly as the customer wishes. Some customers don't mind if you're a few days late. Others do. So, if on occasion, you're a few days late, inform your customers about it. They will appreciate you for being considerate enough to advise them of the temporary delay.

Here are a few other helpful suggestions about dealing with customers. Always be polite. And do a good job of mowing without missing any areas of the lawn. Stick to these simple rules and eventually you will have many customers.

EPILOGUE

When writing this book, I decided to show only 11 of John's customers as example mowing jobs. He actually had many other customers. To have shown all of his customers would have been overwhelming to any unfamiliar individual just getting started in the mowing business.

The 11 customers that were shown were selected because they provided the range of particular sizes of properties and associated prices to prove the point that you can make the biggest money by mowing the smallest lawns. Eleven also turned out to be an acceptable number of customers for another reason.

You will recall that, as a part of the central theme of the book, the emphasis was placed on a "one-man operation working on a part-time basis." By taking this approach to the business, the average high school student, or anyone older, could feel comfortable with serving only 11 customers (assuming, of course, that all the properties are smaller than one-third of an acre). Anyone can handle 11 customers (with small lawns) in about seven or eight hours a week.

However, if someone wants to hustle, working harder and longer hours, it's possible to serve 25 or 30 customers, alone, on a part-time basis and more. This leads us to the question of just how many customers one person can handle. So here's the rest of the story:

When John had become well experienced and worked real hard, while at his peak, he mowed lawns for as many as 50 customers.

Here is the progression of events, over a period of five mowing seasons, which tells how he built up to serving 50 customers.

During John's first mowing season in 1980, when he was 14 years of age, he mowed the lawns of the 11 example customers, plus a few other customers. During his second mowing season in 1981, when he was 15, he mowed the lawns of the 11 example customers, plus five or six other customers. At this point John had begun to be most effective at all phases of the business.

In his third mowing season in 1982, when he was 16, John was mowing lawns for 20 customers. He could have mowed lawns for additional customers, but leveled off at this point. He was satisfied with the balance between his obligated part-time hours and his earned income. The most noticeable change during this season was a more mature approach to the business. John focused principally upon mowing just those lawns that required an hour or less of mowing time -- the prime jobs, where he was earning $12.00 to $14.00 an hour. He maintained this focus hereafter.

During the fourth mowing season in 1983, when John was 17, he was mowing lawns for 35 customers. He was more ambitious during this mowing season; he wanted to buy a car and date girls. This was a demanding workload for him. In the months of May and June there were periods when he was hard pressed to mow all of the lawns alone. Therefore, he hired a friend to help him for an average of about $5.00 a lawn. (This was a new growth that opened John's eyes to a higher level in the business world, seeing how to increase his rate of income by using hired help.)

During John's fifth, and last, mowing season in 1984, when he was 18, he was mowing lawns for 50 customers. This was an enormous task. At this point, he was working a full-time job during his after school hours. In the months of May and June he worked nearly every day after school and on weekends (except when it rained). And, with the experience gained from the previous season using hired help, he had two, and sometimes three, different friends working for him. When school was out for the summer, he was able to handle all these customers alone, as a fulltime job. And, during his best weeks, he was earning nearly $ 1,000.00 per week.

The following year he enlisted in the U. S. Air Force and honorably served his country for four years. He is now a Christian minister and he also operates two businesses (as mentioned in the Author's Notes).

ROBERT A. WELCOME.

Printed in the United States
138707LV00002B/45/P